Especially for

....

From

....

Date

....

Discovering God in
Everyday Moments

180 Devotions
for Women

Janet Ramsdell Rockey

BARBOUR BOOKS
An Imprint of Barbour Publishing, Inc.

© 2015 by Barbour Publishing, Inc.

Print ISBN 978-1-62836-913-7

eBook Editions:
Adobe Digital Editions (.epub) 978-1-63409-142-8
Kindle and MobiPocket Edition (.prc) 978-1-63409-143-5

Published by Barbour Books, an imprint of Barbour Publishing, Inc., P.O. Box 719, Uhrichsville, Ohio 44683, www.barbourbooks.com

Our mission is to publish and distribute inspirational products offering exceptional value and biblical encouragement to the masses.

Member of the
Evangelical Christian
Publishers Association

Printed in the United States of America.

Introduction

EXAMINING THE SCRIPTURES—ACTS 17:11

Blessings come when we least expect them. In a recent prayer, I mentioned my desire to learn more about God's Word. I wanted to pore over the scriptures to understand the premise of each of the sixty-six books. But a full time job, family needs, and writing a novel left little time for this depth of study. I set my Bible-learning goal on a back burner, along with other "someday" projects.

The Lord pushed it right back to the front burner and turned the dial to high heat. The editor at Barbour Publishing asked me to contribute to their project, *Prayers a Faithful Heart*. That sweet assignment compelled me to examine Ephesians, preparing me for His next blessing. After I turned in my thirteen prayers, she asked me to write this devotional, using all sixty-six books of the Bible. I've studied each book to ensure my everyday moments matched the context of the selected verses.

God answered my prayer with a bonus. Not only has He granted me this opportunity to dig through His Word, but I can also share what I've learned with you.

He truly is in everyday moments.

—Janet Ramsdell Rockey

Discovering God In Music

VIOLIN DUET

*Praise Him with timbrel and dancing; Praise Him with
stringed instruments and pipe. Praise Him with loud cymbals;
Praise Him with resounding cymbals. Let everything that
has breath praise the L*ORD*. Praise the L*ORD*!*
PSALM 150:4–6 NASB

Twenty-one-year-old Grace stood on the platform next to her
younger brother, David. They picked up their violins and gently
placed them on their shoulders. Pressing their fingers down on the
strings, they drew their bows firmly to create the violins' haunting
voices. Their wrists quivered with just the right intensity as they
played the time-honored hymn. With each rise and fall of the bow,
a joyful noise floated toward heaven, lifting my concerns.

The psalms tell us repeatedly to praise the Lord with musical
instruments. A young shepard named David soothed the tortured
soul of a king with the sweet sounds of music. Every time he played
his harp, the evil spirit departed from Saul, taking the king's distress
with it.

The Lord bestowed a wonderful gift on these two young
violinists. Like the psalmist, their training and talent played out on
their stringed instruments calms our souls and causes us to praise
God for His blessings.

TRUMPETS

God has gone up with a shout,
*the L*ORD *with the sound of a trumpet.*
PSALM 47:5 NKJV

Our church organist played the dramatic notes of Jeremiah Clarke's "Trumpet Voluntary," weaving a tapestry of majestic tones throughout the sanctuary. Able to duplicate other musical instruments, the digital organ produced a full symphony of strings, reeds, and percussion to deliver this heavenly composition.

Clarke composed this work in 1700 for Britain's Queen Anne and her new husband. Many brides, including the late Princess Diana, have marched down the aisle to the sounds of this classical piece. The trumpets' regal blasts, followed by the commanding melody, create music worthy of royalty.

Almighty God is the exalted King who ascends to the heavens and sits on His throne of holiness. But He loved us enough to descend to earth from His heavenly abode to be born in the form of a perfect man, Jesus. He died, rose from the dead, and ascended into heaven, providing a clear path for us to our heavenly Father.

Each time our church organist plays "Trumpet Voluntary," my heart soars with joy, and I thank the Lord for the anticipated trumpet announcement of Jesus Christ's imminent return.

A SONG IN MY HEART

*Speaking to yourselves in psalms and hymns
and spiritual songs, singing and making
melody in your heart to the Lord.*
EPHESIANS 5:19 KJV

The apostle Paul encouraged new believers in Ephesus to honor the Lord with their songs. What makes up a song? A combination of musical notes produces the melody. Words convey the message. When we put these together, we have composed a lyrical tune.

But there is more to a song than lyrics and melody. Although these elements are needed, a song must have rhythm. Rhythm is the heartbeat of the song. Without the methodical tempo, the music flounders and falls flat. The rhythm pulses the song's essence through its musical scale the same way our hearts pump blood through our veins.

The heart needs rhythm to give it time to rest between contractions. Without those pauses, it wears out and dies. Without pauses in music, the song flat-lines into a lifeless, empty mantra.

In giving us rhythm for our music and lives, our Creator has put His song in our hearts. May our music return to Him with a richness that brings honor to His glorious name.

Discovering God In Leisure Activities

REST AND REGENERATE

There remains a Sabbath rest for the people of God.
For the one who has entered His rest has himself also
rested from his works, as God did from His.
HEBREWS 4:9–10 NASB

We live in a non-stop, "24/7" society that urges us to rush in everything we do. "If you snooze, you lose" is our culture's motto.

But God wants us to rest. Giving ourselves a period of relaxation allows us to regenerate. With the barrier of stress and fatigue knocked down, our objective views, logical solutions, and creative ideas flow through us again.

The same is true spiritually. God modeled this standard for us after six days of creation. He calls us to rest in His finished work on our behalf. Our attempts to work for our salvation prove as futile as Adam's fig leaf apron. The Lord invites us to lean on His promise through our complete dependence on Him.

When we put our feet up on a footstool after a long workday, let us remember to also rest from our efforts to prove ourselves worthy of heaven. Through Jesus' finished work on the cross we have the opportunity to enter into God's rest.

READING

*How can a young person stay on the path
of purity? By living according to your word.*
PSALM 119:9 NIV

Mysteries, thrillers, and love stories entertain us with memorable characters in bizarre circumstances. Do-it-yourself and other non-fiction books educate us in politics, health issues, or foreign cultures. Anthologies present short stories for quick reads.

Of all my books, my favorite is filled with true stories of kingdoms, journeys, wars, and love. With sixty-six small books inside a large one, a reader unfamiliar with this work would call it an anthology. But all these books tie in together. It begins with the creation of a perfect world, followed by its downfall, and ends victoriously with everything being restored.

The book is a how-to on life and morals, good for educating us in politics, health issues, and Middle-eastern cultures. It's a mystery, dropping clues to what will come in the future. It's a thriller with good repeatedly overcoming evil. In addition, a love story weaves its way throughout as God reveals how precious we are to Him. He wants us to be pure. How can we attain this? The answer is found in His word—the Bible.

BONFIRES

Shadrach, Meshach and Abed-nego replied to the king,
"O Nebuchadnezzar, we do not need to give you an answer
concerning this matter. If it be so, our God whom we serve
is able to deliver us from the furnace of blazing fire;
and He will deliver us out of your hand, O king."
DANIEL 3:16–17 NASB

On cold nights, our family enjoys a blazing bonfire. We roast
marshmallows or hot dogs and chat with friends. While the fire
heats our fronts, our backsides remain chilled, so every few minutes
we turn to warm the other side. This rotisserie effect wasn't true
of the furnace King Nebuchadnezzar used to punish Shadrach,
Meshach and Abed-nego.

Those young men believed God could save them. But if
He chose not to, they declared that they would continue to
hold true to their faith. In either case, they would be free. Their
fervent love for the Lord and His miraculous deliverance softened
Nebuchadnezzar's heart, and he believed.

The next time we warm ourselves in front of a bonfire, let us
consider these three men whose devotion to God delivered them
from a fiery death. We don't know when our actions and attitudes
could soften someone's heart toward God.

QUILTING

It shall come to pass, that whosoever shall call on the
name of the LORD shall be delivered; for in mount Zion and
in Jerusalem shall be deliverance, as the LORD hath said,
and in the remnant whom the LORD shall call.
JOEL 2:32 KJV

I still treasure the quilts my grandmother made more than forty years ago. She set aside pieces of my outfits to sew into the wedding ring design. Tattered and faded, even now they keep me warm on chilly winter nights. Yet the warmth from these quilts doesn't compare to my cozy memories of Grandmother Mary Belle. She is with Christ now, but her quilting creations remain as a tribute of her love.

In a similar way, the Lord set aside a remnant of His people when Israel was taken into captivity. These faithful few kept His laws and shunned the false idols others worshipped.

God promises He will deliver another faithful remnant in the last days; a people set aside because of their unwavering belief. If He were to create a heavenly quilt from His remnants, perhaps He would use the wedding ring pattern. What a lovely tribute of His eternal love!

MENDING

*"Yet even now," declares the LORD, "return to Me with
all your heart, and with fasting, weeping and mourning;
and rend your heart and not your garments."*
JOEL 2:12–13 NASB

When one of my favorite outfits has a split seam, I choose thread
that matches the torn garment and then select the right needle.
Sometimes I use special mending tape if the fabric is too frayed to
hold a stitch. My careful patchwork may hide the tear for a while,
but the garment will never be as strong as before. Nevertheless, torn
clothing is easier to mend than a wounded heart.

To the early Israelites, ripping their garments indicated deep
regret. The Lord asked them to rend their hearts; symbolizing the
most profound remorse possible, accompanied by fasting, weeping,
and mourning.

Even today, when we stray from God's path of righteousness,
all He asks is that we return to Him with a contrite heart, mind, and
soul. His abundant love does more than patch a heart ripped open
by regret. His mercy restores it to the strength it had before. We are
His, patched and mended, because of His great love for us.

AN ARTIST'S PAINTING

Behold, He who forms mountains and creates the
wind and declares to man what are His thoughts, He who
makes dawn into darkness and treads on the high places
of the earth, The LORD God of hosts is His name.
AMOS 4:13 NASB

Original paintings of renowned artists are expensive, but an artist's signature dramatically increases its value. That's why galleries employ experts to spot forgeries. They are trained to know the artist's techniques, even the formation of the signature.

God's work contains no forgeries or prints. He has painted majestic mountains with plums and browns, then finished them off with snowy white tops. Streaks of red, yellow, and violet spread like fingers in a sunset. Mixed tones of gold, green, and tan blanket the earth. He sprinkled the meadows with flowers of bright red and hushed lavender. He colored the oceans in deep blues and the seas in soft turquoise. Tiny lights twinkle in the inky-blackness of the night sky.

Look upon God's creation. Behold His artistry. He has illustrated His omnipotence like a portrait and signed His name to it.

CAMPING

Moses used to set up a tent far from camp.
He called it the "meeting tent," and whoever needed
some message from the LORD would go there.
EXODUS 33:7 CEV

Camp counselors supervise large groups of children from six to eighteen years old. They entertain the youngsters with stories, games, and songs. Protecting them from dangerous wild animals, biting insects, and poisonous plant life falls under the job description, too.

Campers come to them for all sorts of reasons—a skinned knee, bruised ego, or broken heart—and the counselors are ready with a bandage, a kind word, or a spiritual hug. As leaders, these young men and women have the opportunity to be the Moses of the campground.

Moses served as the camp counselor for the Israelites in the wilderness. But he did more than bandage their wounds and provide encouragement. He consulted with God on their behalf and gave them godly counsel.

Although camp counselors spend a few short weeks with children, they still have opportunities to lead these adolescents in the ways of the Lord. Like Moses, they pitch their tents in the wilderness and wait for God's counsel.

HIKING

*The Lord God is my strength, and He has made my
feet like hinds' feet, and makes me walk on my high places.*
HABAKKUK 3:19 NASB

Seasoned hikers trek across rocky paths and overgrown trails with
a developed second nature. They take in the sights and sounds of
the natural environment around them, unshaken by steep cliffs
and rubble-strewn paths. They glide up one side of a mountain and
down the other with surefooted confidence.

Our heavenly Father frees us from dread of danger as we scale
the rugged terrain of our lives. We can hike our trails of uncertainty
with surefooted confidence putting our trust in Him.

The prophet Habakkuk looked to God for strength despite
the approaching invasion of the Chaldeans. He trusted the Lord to
remember His mercy in the midst of His wrath against the Israelites.
He trusted the Lord to keep them from falling to their enemies.

God is with us, in comfort and distress. When we stumble, in
His mercy He will pick us up, strengthen us, and set us back on our
feet.

DEEP SEA FISHING

He saith unto them, "Follow me,
and I will make you fishers of men."
MATTHEW 4:19 KJV

The "one that got away" is a favorite story for many deep-sea fishermen. With every telling, the size of the escapee gets longer and wider. It might end well for the fish that took the bait and not the hook, but it isn't a happy ending for the one that got away when we don't share the Gospel of Jesus Christ.

Jesus called Simon Peter and his brother, Andrew, into His ministry because they knew how to catch fish. He asked them to leave their nets and follow Him so that He could teach them to catch people instead. Without hesitation, they did just that and became two of the twelve Jesus chose to be His disciples.

Today, Jesus is calling us to do just what Peter and Andrew did—bait our hooks with the love of Christ and reel in new believers for the Kingdom of God. There are still a lot of fish in the sea. There are too many who have not heard His message of eternal life. Let's get back to fishing.

CAST NET FISHING

Simon answered and said, "Master, we worked hard all night and caught nothing, but I will do as You say and let down the nets." When they had done this, they enclosed a great quantity of fish, and their nets began to break.

LUKE 5:5-6 NASB

I watched a fisherman cast his net and then pull it back up empty. It reminded me of my own unsuccessful attempts to overcome a challenge. How often do we repeat fruitless endeavors before going to the Lord? Why do we continue casting our nets when they return to us empty?

Simon Peter had fished all night and caught nothing. When Jesus told him to go into the deep water, Peter knew the conditions he needed for a catch were not in place. Yet he believed Jesus. His obedience to Christ's directive, in spite of his weariness, resulted in so great a catch that his boat almost sank.

The Lord's solution requires perseverance. We might question the logic of His prompting, but He is the creator of all wisdom. When we trust and obey Him, He will fill our nets with His abundance.

SAVE THE DATE

Do not let this one fact escape your notice, beloved,
that with the Lord one day is like a thousand years,
and a thousand years like one day.
2 PETER 3:8 NASB

Save the Date is a popular new tradition. When we mark the
calendar for an anticipated happy occasion, it often feels like an
eternity will pass before the joyful event occurs. Then, the day
arrives, and it's all over in a flash. We sweep up the confetti, bridal
rice, or tickertape and return to our regular lives.

Two thousand years have passed since Peter wrote about
Christ's anticipated return. But it's only been a day in heaven,
maybe two. We cannot comprehend God's calendar. Infinity is a
mystery to us. Although He dwells in eternity, God created time for
us here on earth.

We can't save the date for Christ's return because no one but
God knows when that will be. We must trust Him to save the date
for us. However, unlike our anticipated happy occasions here on
earth, this glorious event won't be over in a flash. We will join the
King of kings and that glorious day will last forever.

OUR GODLY HERITAGE

The word of the Lord which came unto Zephaniah the son of Cushi,
the son of Gedaliah, the son of Amariah, the son of Hizkiah,
in the days of Josiah the son of Amon, king of Judah.
ZEPHANIAH 1:1 KJV

After searching through some musty family records, I found my
dad's Army Air Corps pilot's flight log, a treasure that told a story
of WWII. My great-grandparents' tattered marriage certificate
suggested a romantic elopement, and I saw a family resemblance in
the eyes of an infant featured in a yellowed photo. Advertisements
are everywhere encouraging us to use their websites to trace our
roots.

Biblical genealogies show us that God does place importance
on family lineage. We learn that Zephaniah was a descendant of
the good King Hezekiah, for example. However, we should recognize
that we have a spiritual ancestry as well. Who told us about the
love of Christ? Who told that person?

Let's give thanks for the friend, family member, or stranger
who told us about Christ or prayed for us when we were lost.
Perhaps one day, someone will give thanks that our words and
actions helped them discover their godly heritage.

SCRAPBOOKING

Those who feared the LORD spoke to one another, and the LORD gave attention and heard it, and a book of remembrance was written before Him for those who fear the LORD and who esteem His name.
MALACHI 3:16 NASB

Storing precious memories in scrapbooks has become a contemporary art form. We use specific tools to crop out unwanted clutter from our photographs and then cut the picture to fit a contoured frame. We decorate each page with themed decals and ornate trim and then top it off with a dialogue box. A picture may be worth a thousand words, but journaling on the photo page keeps the memory fresh.

Malachi didn't need a snapshot of the faithful to put into an elaborate album. God knew who they were. He valued them as a special treasure because they feared Him and esteemed His name.

God has cropped out our transgressions and framed us to fit on an embellished page in His book of remembrance. And the dialogue box reads: "These are Mine, and I will spare them."

USING A VENDING MACHINE

God promised Abraham and his descendants that he would give
them the world. This promise wasn't made because Abraham had
obeyed a law, but because his faith in God made him acceptable.
ROMANS 4:13 CEV

We insert money into a vending machine, push the right button,
and watch the chosen snack drop into the tray. Sadly, some
people think God's blessings come that way. If they put in a bit
of obedience, they expect a smidgen of blessing. But God simply
doesn't work that way. He wants our hearts more than our empty,
dutiful acts.

Throughout his wanderings, Abraham never wavered in his
faith. When God told him he would have a son in his old age,
Abraham believed that God would keep His promises. He didn't
expect God to dispense blessings in exchange for his obedience, but
because he was faithful.

We are God's children and heirs to His blessings. These
blessings come to us not because of what we do but because of
who He is.

Discovering God In The Courtroom

KEEPING THE LAW

We know that the Law is good, if one uses it lawfully.
1 Timothy 1:8 NASB

Our court system enforces the laws our governing authorities enact. These civil laws were created to maintain order. We admit our failure to comply when we go to court to pay a fine or give a defense for a lapse in sound judgment.

In God's courtroom, the laws are designed to remind us that we are flawed and can only prosper and live blessed lives as we abide under the authority of our heavenly Father's Kingdom. But too often, we distort God's commands and twist His statutes with vague interpretations in order to justify our inadequacies. Doing this undermines God's ability to protect and bless us.

In a similar manner, breaking civil laws or treating them with disrespect lessens their ability to bless and protect us. In both cases, however, accepting responsibility for our words and actions demonstrates our willingness to live orderly lives, while respecting God's authority and receiving the benefits our God-centered lives afford.

Discovering God In Caring For Our Pets

THE PURR OF CONTENTMENT

I have learned the secret of living in every situation, whether it is with a full stomach or empty, with plenty or little.
PHILIPPIANS 4:12 NLT

Cats seem to know that true contentment doesn't depend on external conditions. They have the uncanny ability to make a rutted tree log appear as comfortable as a velvet cushion. They contort their bodies into positions that would baffle a pretzel maker just to fit inside an odd-shaped box. And then they purr. But even a happy cat will demand food at mealtime.

In his letter to the Christians at Philippi, Paul explains that hardship isn't a sign of God's displeasure. Being in need teaches us to rely completely on the Lord's provision. By the same token, we can't claim His approval when we prosper—for that, too, must stay within the context of His providing hand.

God's Word reveals the secret of being satisfied in all circumstances. If we seek His will, He will strengthen us in every situation. This level of contentment surpasses even that of a happy, purring cat.

CHESSIE THE KITTEN

You will rest safe and secure, filled with hope and emptied of worry.
JOB 11:18 CEV

An etching of a kitten asleep under the covers captured the attention of Chesapeake Railroad officials. The image of the kitten they named Chessie became the epitome of peaceful rest. They used it to advertise that their passenger train offered a smoother ride than any of the others. The scripture above might have served as their slogan. It certainly expressed peace and rest in the midst of Job's turbulent circumstances.

As Job suffered loss after tragic loss, his friends presumed God was punishing him. They offered Job the hope of undisturbed rest if he would repent. Not only was their analysis wrong, but that promise was not theirs to make. Only God could extend that assurance.

Job was a man of integrity, devoted to his Creator. Even when his wife suggested cursing God, he maintained his faith. God eventually restored Job, giving him long-desired rest.

We can curl up under God's coverlet like Chessie and rely on His promise of rest that is safe and secure. Our journey won't always be smooth, but it'll be filled with hope and emptied of worry.

PUPPY LOVE

Blessed are those who trust in the LORD and have made the LORD their hope and confidence.
JEREMIAH 17:7 NLT

The trust and adoration a young puppy has for his master is evident as he stares up into his master's face. After all, the young dog can't buy a bag of his favorite kibble. He relies on his human for food, shelter, and love. And if not for his master's home, he would be at the pound or, worse, living in danger on the streets.

Just like the puppy depends on his master, we must depend on God. Our own strength is imperfect and destined to fail. We would be foolish to rely on money, fame, or a certain religion or political system. We can't even depend on our own bodies and minds. All but God will disappoint us in the end.

Once we learn what the puppy knows instinctively, we will look to God with grateful eyes and trusting hearts, understanding that He is the source of all provisions in our lives.

Discovering God In Vehicles

ROADBLOCK

A lazy person's way is blocked with briers, but the path of the upright is an open highway.
PROVERBS 15:19 NLT

Most all of us find ourselves caught up in a traffic jam from time to time. We know what it's like to sit there and watch impatient drivers speed by, cutting in front of those who are graciously waiting their turn. Sometimes, though, a semi-truck driver will take the initiative and pull out of the stopped lane, straddling the white lines. This temporarily blocks the impatient drivers and opens the way for us.

Sometimes we encounter traffic jams in our faith. Skeptics seem to enjoy trying to block us in and provoke a negative response. When this happens, the Bible says we should wait patiently for the Lord's help. He will provide truth, wisdom, and understanding to straddle the white line and shut down the skeptics. Then He will show us how to get our faith flowing again.

Once we learn to depend on Him, we can relax and respond in a positive manner to the skeptics in our lives.

OVERHEATED RADIATOR

My cup runneth over.
PSALM 23:5 KJV

When the temperature gauge needle moves to the big red *H*, it's time to pull the car to the side of the road and immediately turn off the ignition. The warning light means that our engine needs water—right away! Without enough water in the radiator, the pressure rises and what's left is ready to blow. We must wait for it to equalize before opening it. Otherwise, the super-heated water inside will erupt at the turn of the valve, with tragic results.

Without the living water Jesus offers, we overheat, too. When we tackle the demands of work, family, or other issues by ourselves, our pressure builds. When someone innocently releases our valve, we often erupt in anger.

While it's prudent to frequently check fluid levels in our car engines, maintaining our spiritual levels is even more important. Jesus wants us to give Him our burdens. When we trade our troubles for His peace, our cups will overflow with living water instead of exploding in a steaming rage.

THE BLOWOUT

It came to pass in an eveningtide, that David arose from off his bed, and walked upon the roof of the king's house; and from the roof he saw a woman washing herself; and the woman was very beautiful to look upon.

2 SAMUEL 11:2 KJV

A blown tire can be frightening. As we steer our limping car out of the traffic flow, we wonder how it happened. Even with carefully maintained tires, a sharp object on the road can do damage. It must be taken care of before we can get back on the highway and continue our journey.

In the same way, sin can creep into the life of the most devout believer and cause a spiritual blowout. This happened to King David as he stood on the rooftop of his palace one evening. From there, he saw a beautiful woman bathing, which led to adultery and murder. The damage was great, but repentance, and God's forgiveness, put him back on the road again.

We must watch for the debris of temptation on the road of our lives by focusing on the Lord and His Word. But when the worst happens, our heavenly Father assures us of His mercy.

LET'S NOT MEET BY ACCIDENT

*If you forgive others for their transgressions,
your heavenly Father will also forgive you.*
Matthew 6:14 NASB

No one chooses to be in an auto accident. Inclement weather can create hazardous road conditions, which make driving difficult. A heavy fog limits our vision in front and behind us. And who can stop suddenly without skidding on wet, slippery pavement? Even in pleasant weather, one small error in judgment or a brief distraction or a slip of the foot to the wrong pedal can result in a multiple-car collision.

When on the receiving end of an accident, let us not fly into a rage. The other car suffered damage, too. God wants us to show mercy to the person who caused the fender-bender. A gentle response is a reflection of God's character. He has provided us with the ability to forgive because He forgave our transgressions through Jesus Christ.

When the fault is ours, let us demonstrate humility, freely admitting our fault, taking responsibility, and asking for forgiveness. Those we meet by accident might discover God in us through a potentially unpleasant situation.

ARE WE THERE YET?

I have traveled on many long journeys. I have faced danger.
2 CORINTHIANS 11:26 NLT

Long-distance road trips create weary travelers. Hour after hour the countryside zips past while we keep pace with the traffic flow. When we stop for quick refreshments and to refill the gas tank, the inevitable question arises, "Are we there yet?"

The apostle Paul's account of his arduous journeys to the church at Corinth describes more difficult travel than we have probably encountered. He was beaten, stoned, and shipwrecked along the way. And yet, he was certain of the purpose for this trip—to encourage new believers in the faith—and that was more important to him than any suffering he endured.

The journeys we take to fulfill God's purpose in our lives can also be long and difficult. But God assures us that everything He asks us to do is of great importance. And when we arrive, we won't have to ask, "Are we there yet?" We'll behold God's radiant glory.

RACING CHARIOTS

The chariots race recklessly along the streets and rush
wildly through the squares. They flash like firelight
and move as swiftly as lightning.
NAHUM 2:4 NLT

Race cars zoom past their fans in a roaring flash. Drivers try to
out-maneuver each other, weaving in and out of tight spaces on
the oval track. Round and round they go, to nowhere, but getting
there fast.

We've all experienced similar moments in our lives—going in
circles without making progress. We need frequent pit stops to take
a deep breath and view our circumstances with an objective eye.
The evil one promotes unending hurry. He would drive our days
without rest so we forget to call on the Lord during times of need.

God won't ask us to drive chariots through the streets of
Nineveh to destroy His enemy, but He will invite us into His pit stop
for peace during our hectic moments. We can stop racing in circles
and take a quiet ride on His straight and narrow path.

REAL WEALTH

When you become successful, don't say, "I'm rich,
and I've earned it all myself." Instead, remember that
the LORD your God gives you the strength to make a living.
DEUTERONOMY 8:17–18 CEV

Riches don't impress the Lord. Why would they? All wealth comes from His hand to begin with. He can give a vast fortune and snatch it away just as easily. He created everything we have, and it all belongs to Him.

Instead of seeking to be rich, we should consider what an honor it is to serve as ambassadors for God's kingdom. As believers in Christ, we have a treasure in God's abiding love. And that's a treasure we can depend on. True riches that will never fail us.

Moses admonished the Israelites in the wilderness to not let wealth become their idol when they entered the Promised Land. His warning applies to us, too. Let us pursue God's riches in Glory instead. As His ambassadors, we have the protection of God's diplomatic immunity, if not in this mortal life, then in the kingdom to come. We can rest comfortably in His assurance and hope.

REMOVING RUBBISH

Since we have so great a cloud of witnesses surrounding us,
let us also lay aside every encumbrance and the
sin which so easily entangles us.
HEBREWS 12:1 NASB

Every week, we load containers with unwanted papers and rubbish and set them out for removal. The rumbling garbage truck arrives, with comforting regularity, as early as six o'clock in the morning.

Throwing out useless trash is easy, but culling through stored possessions isn't. We uncover a cherished trinket, now broken. Should we have it repaired or let it go? We ponder an unfamiliar item. A Christmas gift? Maybe a birthday? From whom? Do we dare toss it?

When it comes to spiritual things, it's easy enough to recognize and throw out the obvious sins and undesirable thoughts. But what about the less obvious, sometimes even cherished, thoughts and habits that we hang on to? The Bible instructs us to discard anything that hinders our faith. Our heavenly Father supplies the courage and strength we need to do just that.

When the garbage truck rumbles past, let us ask the Lord to untangle those stubborn encumbrances. Only He can haul them away.

Discovering God In Our Travels

TRAIN TRAVEL

Be careful to do as the LORD your God has commanded you;
you are not to turn aside to the right or the left.
DEUTERONOMY 5:32 HCSB

As we board the train, the conductor checks our tickets to be sure we are headed for the right destination. With the rails firmly in place, the train can only go where the tracks take it. There can be no deviation. Isn't our way to heaven similar?

The station where we board our celestial train is our faith foundation—the place where we came to believe in Jesus. He purchased our tickets for us and marked them, PAID IN FULL. Then Christ, the conductor, checks our tickets to make sure we're on the train going to heaven.

The railroad track represents the Holy Spirit, who keeps the train from turning aside to the right or the left. We must still be alert, listening to His promptings as the Holy Spirit guards against derailing distractions.

As Moses recalled the consuming awesomeness of God's holiness at Sinai, let us consider the power of the locomotive with Almighty God driving it.

Destination: heaven.

THE WILD BLUE YONDER

*According to His promise we are looking for new heavens
and a new earth, in which righteousness dwells.*
2 PETER 3:13 NASB

When airliners go through turbulent storms en route to their
destinations, the window seat (often considered the best for
viewing purposes) subjects the passenger to an alarming display
of clashing air masses and ominous, rolling clouds. The passenger
in the aisle seat (coveted for extra leg room) finds himself pitched
sideways, tethered only by his seat belt and colliding with anyone or
anything in the aisle. But the person in the center (often considered
the least desirable seat) can find comfort in being hemmed in,
seemingly protected from the extremes.

 In the new heavens, however, should there be airliners, it won't
matter what seat we choose. Turbulent flights will be a thing of
the past. As God replaces everything in His creation that sin has
corrupted, all the earth will operate in perfect harmony. Everyone
will be clamoring for the window seat where they can look down at
a landscape even more beautiful than they could have imagined.

SEA CRUISE

*He went to the seaport of Joppa and bought a ticket
on a ship that was going to Spain. Then he got on
the ship and sailed away to escape.*
JONAH 1:3 CEV

Cruise ships were once no more than a means of transportation.
Now they're floating four-star hotels with gourmet meals and
round-the-clock entertainment. The ports of call range from exotic
tropical paradises to the frozen glaciers in Alaska. Cruises offer a
pampered vacation, where almost every whim is granted.

We can set aside our everyday jobs, household tasks, and other
obligations while lounging in a deck chair. But Jonah didn't enjoy
a lavish vacation when he boarded a certain ship to Spain. He ran
away from the Lord in anger, fear, and frustration. Through his
experience, he learned that no one can escape the presence of the
Lord.

As we board the cruise ship for a pleasant escape, let us
remember Jonah. We can't take a vacation from the Lord's presence
either. We see Him in the scenery, the terrain, and the people. Like
Jonah, we can share the love of Christ with the natives in the port
of call.

VACANCY IS A GOOD SIGN

Don't hesitate to accept hospitality, because
those who work deserve to be fed.
MATTHEW 10:10 NLT

Vacancy signs welcome tired travelers. They represent a comfortable bed and, possibly, a hot meal. With the increase of vacationers in today's marketplace, hospitality has grown into a huge industry. However, as motels offer more than a place to sleep, the price rises.

Jesus sent out His twelve disciples to preach the kingdom of heaven to the Jewish people. He gave all of them authority to drive out unclean spirits and heal every kind of sickness. They were to travel light, taking no money or additional clothing. Instead of the local inn, they depended on the hospitality of devout Jewish families.

Today's traveling evangelists also need a safe place to stay and meals to sustain them. They rely on support from other believers. Working through churches and bona fide ministries, we can offer a room, home-cooked food, and financial assistance as they come through our towns.

They are workers for God's kingdom. Let's put out the Vacancy sign and welcome them.

ALL INN THE FAMILY

*Be hospitable to one another without complaining. Based
on the gift each one has received, use it to serve others,
as good managers of the varied grace of God.*
1 PETER 4:9-10 HCSB

Sometimes we rely on family hospitality when we travel. Being a
gracious guest means adjusting to our hosts' activities while staying
in their homes. They rearrange their schedules to accommodate our
wishes, show us regional sights, or treat us to lunch at their favorite
restaurant.

Considering ways to please our hosts, we compliment their
home and neighborhood. As a gift of service, we offer to prepare a
meal and clean up. If our physical capabilities allow, we'll join them
in their morning walk routine. If they enjoy sitting in the backyard,
we relax with them. The Bible urges us to use whatever God has
given us to bless those who open their homes to us.

We portray God's grace to our family members when we take
the time to encourage and strengthen them when they open their
homes and lives to us.

Discovering God In Holidays And Events

A NEW BEGINNING

The LORD has taken away His judgments against you, He has
cleared away your enemies. The King of Israel, the LORD, is in
your midst; you will fear disaster no more. . . I will save the
lame and gather the outcast, and I will turn their shame
into praise and renown in all the earth.
ZEPHANIAH 3:15, 19 NASB

On New Year's Day, we often make resolutions. Turning over a
new leaf means giving up an unhealthy habit or starting that
new diet. . .again.

This is a season to plan new beginnings. We face forward, not
backward; yet we don't ignore past mistakes. We can't go back in time to
change them, but they can become teaching moments for the future.

For example, we can move forward in our relationships as we
forgive those who have offended us and ask forgiveness of those
who have reason to be offended by us.

We can be confident that, with the Lord's help, we can
celebrate new beginnings by releasing old patterns and walking in
new ones.

THE GOOD NEWS OF GOOD FRIDAY

*He was pierced through for our transgressions, He was
crushed for our iniquities; the chastening for our well-being
fell upon Him, and by His scourging we are healed.*

Isaiah 53:5 NASB

The day our Savior was crucified is a solemn day, but one that
points the way to true joy. Christ's death fulfilled Scripture, the first
of many, by being the blood sacrifice made by God for Adam and
Eve. Even in the ram sent to spare Isaac's life. In that tense moment,
the ram's head caught in a thicket, indicating the crown of thorns
Jesus would bear.

Isaiah's prophecy distinctly details the wounds from the
whippings and beatings. Christ's hands and feet were pierced as
the soldiers nailed Him to the cross, and a sword pierced His side to
prove He was dead.

Yes, Jesus suffered a horrible death to rid us of our sins. The
good news is His blood doesn't merely cover our sin, as the blood
of the animal did for Adam and Eve. It washes away any trace of
it. Because of Christ's shed blood, we enter the presence of our
heavenly Father.

Praise God for His sacrificial love and blessed forgiveness.

HE IS RISEN INDEED

*"He is not here, but He has risen. Remember how He spoke
to you while He was still in Galilee, saying that the Son of Man
must be delivered into the hands of sinful men,
and be crucified, and the third day rise again."*

LUKE 24:6–7 NASB

The tomb, though sealed and guarded, could not stand against God's almighty power.

The heavy stone rolled away by the angel, not to set Jesus free, but to prove He had risen, could not stand against God's almighty power.

The Roman guards, struck dumb at the angels' presence, could not stand against God's almighty power.

The burial wrappings, holding the shape and position of His absent body, could not stand against God's almighty power.

Without this fulfillment of prophecy in Scripture, we have no hope. The phrase, "He is risen" is the foundation of our Christian faith.

The day we observe Christ's resurrection is more important than the day of His birth. On Resurrection Day we celebrate our own second birth. Let us rejoice and be glad that this is the Day the Lord has made.

Through God's almighty power, Christ is risen indeed.

MEMORIAL DAY

Even the LORD God of hosts; the LORD is his memorial.
Therefore turn thou to thy God: keep mercy and judgment
and wait on thy God continually.
HOSEA 12:5–6 KJV

The observance of Memorial Day, previously called Decoration Day, came about when Southern widows decorated the graves of soldiers who had died in the "War Between the States." Those Christian ladies showed neither favoritism nor bitterness, placing flowers on the resting places of Union and Confederate fathers, husbands, brothers, and sons. All these men were willing to die for a cause, for a principle, for freedom.

God gave great importance to memorials. He set in place specific feasts for His people to commemorate miracles and milestones. The prophet Hosea reminded the Israelites of the most important memorial: the Lord God of Hosts.

In contemporary times, we pay homage to our soldiers from every war—all those who died to preserve our liberty. This Memorial Day, as we honor our fallen soldiers with parades and ceremonies, let us also pay homage to Jesus, who gave His life to save the world. The cross is His memorial.

GOD'S PROMISE OF FREEDOM

The Scriptures declare that we are all prisoners of sin, so we receive
God's promise of freedom only by believing in Jesus Christ.
GALATIANS 3:22 NLT

Every Fourth of July, we celebrate Independence Day with fireworks, picnics, and parades. The fight against British domination was a hard-fought victory. Those who gave their lives to win political freedom believed the result would be worth the sacrifice. As we consider their costly victory, we should ask ourselves: Am I willing to battle imbedded sin to gain eternal freedom?

Our old nature tolerates invisible shackles, which bind us to the dungeon of sin. Daily we struggle against spiritual manacles. We try to obey God's commandments to Moses. Then we discover again and again that His laws mirror our own lost condition. They can't save us, but they can point us to Christ.

Our Father God gives us the strength and wisdom to fight the good fight through belief in Jesus Christ, who fulfills God's promise of liberation from sin's tyranny.

As we celebrate this special day, let us remember this truth: Freedom from another nation's rule is temporal, but freedom in Christ, which God promised, lasts forever.

THE VOICE OF THANKSGIVING

I will sacrifice to You with the voice of thanksgiving; I will
pay what I have vowed. Salvation is of the LORD.
JONAH 2:9 NKJV

Jonah prayed in the belly of the great fish, thanking God in advance for his rescue. The Lord considered Jonah's faithfulness and commanded the fish to spit him out on dry land. Jonah kept his promise to the Lord and preached to Nineveh.

More than two thousand years later, the pilgrims also prayed in their distress. They thanked God in advance, believing He would provide enough to carry them through the approaching winter. He honored their steadfastness and protected them from the harsh conditions they faced. Every November, we remember those devoted adventurers who risked everything to build a new life in a strange land.

These two accounts present opposite settings: Jonah ran from God, but the pilgrims ran to Him. God honored both their prayers. We know from these examples that we can trust in the Lord. His faithfulness encourages us to thank Him first, believing He will grant us favor when we pray in His will. He alone is our salvation.

ADVENT OF CHRIST

The angel said unto them, Fear not: for, behold, I bring you good
tidings of great joy, which shall be to all people. For unto you is
born this day in the city of David a Saviour, which is Christ the Lord.
LUKE 2:10–11 KJV

The lights are dimmed in the church sanctuary. Musicians take their
places near the dais. There might be an orchestra or just a piano; a
choir, a quartet, or a soloist. The pageantry isn't for us, but for the
Christ Child whose lowly birth we celebrate.

Between the Christmas hymns and musical interludes, men
and women of differing ages approach the podium and read
Scriptures. Some verses prophesy of the coming Messiah, while
others share the account of the blessed events as they happened so
long ago: the frightened shepherds, the heavenly host, the tidings
that bring great joy even to us today.

A final hymn accompanies the sharing of light from candle to
candle, each flame touching long enough to ignite the next one. In
like manner the light of Christ illumines our hearts, one flame at a
time. Let us pass on the glow all year long.

O LITTLE TOWN

"As for you, Bethlehem Ephrathah, too little to be among the clans of Judah, from you One will go forth for Me to be ruler in Israel. His goings forth are from long ago, from the days of eternity."
MICAH 5:2 NASB

As Christmas approaches, we decorate our homes with colored lights and nativity scenes. Packages magically appear on our doorsteps. Among the gifts we share are loaves of bread flavored with cinnamon and other spices. We wrap them while fresh, capturing their aroma and flavor. On Christmas Day, bread is a staple for our feasts. We serve rolls, biscuits, or slices cut from a fresh-baked loaf.

Micah prophesied that the King would be born in the fruitful house of bread, for that is what Ephrathah and Bethlehem mean.

Jesus is the Bread of Life. Those who come to Him will not be hungry, and those who believe in Him will never be thirsty. Even His crib was a feeding trough, illustrating His nourishing love.

Christ depicted His sacrifice by a loaf shared with His disciples. May we continue to share the fruitful bread of life, not only at Christmas, but throughout the year.

BIRTHDAY WISHES

Job's sons would take turns preparing feasts in their homes, and
they would also invite their three sisters to celebrate with them.
JOB 1:4 NLT

We enjoy birthdays with family and friends. Cake, ice cream, cards, gifts, and a special song provide a festive ambiance. These gatherings celebrate God's gracious gift of life.

The tradition of a cake with candles was once an offering to a pagan goddess. Today they symbolize the light of life with a candle to represent each year lived. Now served with ice cream, these treats offer a hint of the sweetness we find in a life of obedience to the Lord. The cards, gifts, and song contribute to the wishes of many more birthdays to come.

With each year, we add another candle and another prayer of thanks to the Lord for extending our days on earth. As Job knew all too well, God gives and takes away. As we blow out the candles in one blast of air, let us praise God for each birthday and rejoice. He has given us another year to serve Him.

WEDDING DAY

Let us rejoice and be glad and give the glory to Him, for the
marriage of the Lamb has come and His bride has made herself
ready. It was given to her to clothe herself in fine linen, bright and
clean; for the fine linen is the righteous acts of the saints.
REVELATION 19:7–8 NASB

The radiant bride, dressed in white, moves down the aisle to the
altar. Her groom takes her hand and accepts her as his wife.

The traditional wedding ceremony points to the prophecy of
Christ's return. On that glorious wedding day, the Lamb will accept
the church as His bride. The church is not comprised of a building
or a specific denomination. We, who believe in Christ's sacrificial
death, resurrection, and ascension, will be His bride.

God's holiness is too pure to be in the presence of our
unrighteousness. But Jesus Christ's sacrifice replaces our iniquity
with His righteousness, gaining God's favor for us. We can approach
God's throne with confidence because our sins are washed away.
We come to the Father in purity through the blood of Jesus Christ,
and He loves us more deeply than a bridegroom loves his bride.

HEARTS OF MEMORIES

"My beloved is mine, and I am his."
SONG OF SOLOMON 2:16 NKJV

Whether we've been married one year or fifty, the wedding anniversary is a special time to look back. We reminisce about our courtship and the miraculous way the Lord brought us together. Memories of the big day bring a smile or a chuckle as we relive the moment. We might've had a large wedding, with many bridesmaids and groomsmen, or a small chapel ceremony shared with a chosen few. Even an elopement is worthy of celebration. No matter the size of the happy event, God has ordained this life together.

We promised to love, honor, and cherish each other through every walk of life. In sickness and in health, though rich or poor, for better or for worse, from that day forward, we vowed to forsake all others and keep ourselves only for our beloved spouse.

When we celebrate each anniversary with a reminder of our pledge to each other, then our hearts will be filled with God's love. We can gaze into each other's eyes and say, "My beloved is mine, and I am his."

COMMENCEMENT DAY

*As for every matter of wisdom and understanding about which
the king consulted them, he found them ten times better than
all the magicians and conjurers who were in all his realm.*
DANIEL 1:20 NASB

Daniel, Hananiah, Mishael, and Azariah received the best education
in the land. But they were wiser than their teachers because of their
devout obedience to God. They demonstrated their unyielding faith
early in their captivity under King Nebuchadnezzar. They sought the
Lord and refused to join the magicians or wise men of Babylon.

Pray for our students as they graduate from high school
and college. They need more than an education, more than mere
learning. As they further their education or pursue their careers, let
them have the wisdom to turn away from worldly solutions and
seek God's guidance.

God will lead them when they pray for direction. He will
shield them when they pray for protection, and He will fortify
them when they pray for strength. Let them be ten times wiser
than their teachers and remain steadfast in their faith in the Lord
Jesus Christ.

PRIZE COMPARISON

*I press on toward the goal for the prize of the
upward call of God in Christ Jesus.*
PHILIPPIANS 3:14 NASB

At the Olympics, the winning athletes stand at attention as
an orchestra plays their nation's anthem. It's a grand moment,
crowning years of training for one single purpose: to bring home
the gold.

In Hollywood, even being nominated for an Oscar increases
an actor's desirability for movie roles and more money. How much
more so if they win the coveted award?

But how many Gold Medal athletes or Oscar-winning stars
do we remember years later? We can research the data, but is it
that important? While winning brings us notoriety among our
peers, we know God wants more from us. Relying on our earthly
accomplishments to evaluate our self-worth leaves a void in our
hearts. We feel hollow. Only joy from obeying God's call can fill that
empty space.

All earthly awards pale in comparison to what awaits us in
heaven. We'll press on toward that goal, to hear the Lord say, "Well
done, good and faithful servant."

MAKING MERRY

Celebrate by having parties and by giving to the poor and by sharing gifts of food with each other.
ESTHER 9:22 CEV

Queen Esther and Mordecai had an extraordinary reason to rejoice. God had given them triumph over Haman the Agagite and his plan to destroy the Jewish people. To this day, the descendants of Esther and Mordecai celebrate the Days of Purim every spring.

As Christians, we also commemorate the Lord's conquest on our behalf. Every Sunday reminds us of Christ's victory over death. We meet in a church or a meeting hall for a lesson from the Bible. We sing hymns or praise songs, read scripture verses, and we pray.

Lunch with others may follow the worship service, either at a restaurant or someone's home. We give thanks for the meal and offer praise to the Lord. After discussing and comparing notes of biblical teachings, we have not wearied ourselves of the joyful time spent together in the presence of the Lord. For where two or more are gathered in His name, He is there. And we find that good reason to celebrate.

CROWN JEWELS

The Lord their God will save his people on that day as a shepherd saves his flock. They will sparkle in his land like jewels in a crown.
ZECHARIAH 9:16 NIV

In its rough crystalline form, a diamond is nothing more than a chunk of carbon. It needs to be cut by a faceter before it can disperse light into a rainbow of colors. Whether the stone is meticulously shaped or carefully chipped into dazzling tiny fragments that resemble firelights, a diamond's cut is the most important determinant of its value.

We are God's crown jewels. He is the one who masterfully shapes and chips us to His liking. With divine precision, He painstakingly chisels away the ugly rough spots. He applies heat and pressure for our clarity, and then polishes us until we glisten. He carves in us a gemstone from crude rock to form a jewel worthy of a setting in His crown.

In our transformation, He asks us to wait patiently as He does His work, knowing that in His perfect time we will reflect the firelight of God's brilliance.

VOTING IN ELECTIONS

*Ezra, use the wisdom God has given you and choose officials
and leaders to govern the people of Western Province.
These leaders should know God's laws and have them
taught to anyone who doesn't know them.*
EZRA 7:25 CEV

Many of us dread another election season. Candidates use phone
calls, mailings, and television ads to garner votes. Some sling mud
at their opponents instead of listing their own qualifications. Others
whisper vague rumors to discredit their opponents, ignoring the
important issues. Rarely do we see a clean campaign.

King Artaxerxes recognized the need for God-fearing leaders
to govern the Israelites. He commanded Ezra to select leaders,
knowing the prophet's commitment to God's laws and his nurtured
wisdom for such a task.

Our heavenly Father brought our forefathers to this land to
escape tyranny and establish a new nation. They sought God's
wisdom in writing the Constitution and bringing about our free
elections. They left the Lord's mark in our capitol on various
monuments and memorials.

God has called His children to seek public office. Like Ezra, we
can use the wisdom He gave us to support and elect them, or to get
in the race ourselves.

Discovering God In Weather & Seasons

ENTERTAINING ANGELS

Do not neglect to show hospitality to strangers, for by this some have entertained angels without knowing it.
HEBREWS 13:2 NASB

When a surprise winter storm shut down an entire city, strangers became angels to their fellow motorists.

Black ice on the roads resulted in multiple auto accidents. Instead of ranting about the minimal damage to their cars, people shook hands and offered each other assistance. Drivers provided stranded motorists rides to safety.

Caught in the storm without gloves? A stranger nearby happened to have an extra pair. Can't get to the school to pick up the children? Teachers assured parents the students were safe and warm. Church officials opened their doors to offer hot meals and blankets to people unable to get home; a few even provided cots for an overnight stay.

God calls us to be His messengers in precarious situations. We can help a stranger or let strangers assist us. We won't know if the stranger is an angel or if the presumed angel is a mere human. But God knows. He's right beside us during the storm.

AUTUMN COLORS

Fruit trees of all kinds will grow along both sides of the river.
The leaves of these trees will never turn brown and fall,
and there will always be fruit on their branches.
EZEKIEL 47:12 NLT

Autumn arrives with leaves turning gold, brown, and burgundy. A breeze carries them from their branches to form a mottled carpet on the ground. A picture of beauty covers the sad reality of fall.

Winter is around the corner. Trees draw their sap back into their trunks in preparation for the cold months. The leaves' source of nutrition is cut off. They lose their fresh green color, detach, and fall to the ground.

The Israelites cut themselves off from the nurturing love of God in the autumn of their disbelief. He detached them from the Promised Land and exiled them to Babylon, where they spent the winter of captivity.

We look with hope toward the day when Ezekiel's vision of restoration will come to pass. The Lord's reconciliation will begin as a trickle and then flow as a river of living water. Never again will leaves fall in anticipation of winter. The trees will be forever fruitful in the newness of eternal life.

A BLANKET OF PURITY

"Come, let us discuss this," says the Lord, *"Though your sins are like scarlet, they will be as white as snow; though they are as red as crimson, they will be like wool."*
Isaiah 1:18 HCSB

A night of snow flurries leaves a gift—the untouched beauty of a soft white blanket glistening in the morning light. The surrounding landscape yields its many shapes to the soft wool-like covering. Its quietness hushes the sounds of the awakening day. "Peace, be still," our heavenly Father says to us in this moment of tranquility. Before rushing off to tend to our daily duties, we should take a minute to ponder this image of purity.

The day before, cracked dirt, barren trees, and dead grass revealed the tarnished world in which we live. Our sin nature leaves us broken, unfruitful, and as dry as dead grass. But the Lord Jesus offers the finest solution. When we believe in Him, He washes us in His crimson blood to make us whiter than snow. He will cover us with His purity as we yield ourselves to Him in obedience.

BUDDING PLANTS

Blessed be the God and Father of our Lord Jesus Christ, who according to His great mercy has caused us to be born again to a living hope through the resurrection of Jesus Christ from the dead.
1 PETER 1:3 NASB

Winter vanishes with a hint of color. A nodule appears on a branch. The first brave bud of spring! A sliver of pink surfaces. A future flower slowly emerges after the plant's season of hibernation; an image of living hope through the resurrection of the dead. More sprouts follow. Life returns to the bush.

With the blossoms of new life in the trees, bushes, and ground, the bees and butterflies return. Squirrels and birds come home to build their nests in the flourishing branches.

Our Lord Jesus Christ is the resurrection and the life. As we watch our landscape spring back into life and color, let us give thanks to our Father God, whose plan from the beginning included our rebirth through the resurrection of His Son.

SEEDS IN SUMMER

Those are the ones on whom seed was sown on the good soil;
and they hear the word and accept it and bear fruit,
thirty, sixty, and a hundredfold.
MARK 4:20 NASB

In God's plan, each season has a purpose. Farmers plant their seeds in the spring and then harvest them in the fall. Crops grow and mature in the summer. Without attention during the hot season, they fail to reach maturity in time for the harvest. The farmer can't store his crops for the winter.

In the parable of the sower, Jesus explains why some seeds of His Word fail to mature. Satan steals them away. Worldly desires or fears choke them out. Some have no ground in which to take root.

We need a spiritual summertime to nurture the seeds God has planted in us, as He offers us the warm sunshine of His patience and love. He showers us with the nourishment of good teaching. As our faith matures, we can store His Word in our hearts to support us through the coming spiritual winter. And as we bear fruit, we can help nurture the next crop that God plants.

LIGHTNING

When Solomon finished praying, fire flashed down from heaven and burned up the burnt offerings and sacrifices, and the glorious presence of the LORD filled the Temple.

2 CHRONICLES 7:1 NLT

Lightning—brilliant, instantaneous, and unpredictable—is the most powerful force in the atmosphere. Yet it remains harmless unless it strikes an object. We can't pinpoint its origin. Blinding light flashes from nowhere.

Fire from heaven is God's ultimate expression of His power. His brilliance would blind or consume us if we came face-to-face with Him in our present state. Moses hid in the cleft of a rock to shield himself from God's magnificence.

Although lightning symbolizes God's glorious majesty, enforcing His decrees on those who oppose Him, He didn't use it to destroy those who love Him. His fiery pillar protected and led His people in the wilderness. Fire came down from heaven to accept Elijah's burnt offerings when he challenged the Baal priests, as it did for Solomon when he dedicated the temple.

Like lightning, we can't pinpoint God's origin, for He is eternal. We can't predict when or where He will manifest Himself to us. We can only stand in awe of His power and glory.

THUNDER

The LORD thundered from heaven, and the most
High uttered his voice.
2 SAMUEL 22:14 KJV

Thunder booms like cannon fire in the distance, rolling in closer as the storm approaches. The sudden crash rattles windows and causes large dogs to whine and hide. It sometimes frightens little children. When I was a youngster, I thought the sky was angry. To calm my fears, my father told me the angels were bowling in heaven. He taught me how to keep score as a tactic to settle me down.

The Bible tells us God spoke to His chosen people in thunder. Moses and Job both asserted that His powerful voice roared to them from behind a cloud. David praised the Lord in song, describing His anger in the quaking earth and smoldering coals, and His voice rumbling from the heavens.

The thunderous booms from a storm bring to mind God's commanding voice. But He doesn't speak to us through the clouds anymore. Today, He reaches out to us through His Word, available for us to open and read.

APRIL SHOWERS

"Let us press on to know the LORD. His going forth is as certain as the dawn; and He will come to us like the rain, like the spring rain watering the earth."

HOSEA 6:3 NASB

Rain brings nutrients to our flowers, plants, and crops. It supplies drinking water for mankind and animals, and cleanses dust and pollen from the air and surfaces. Most importantly, it brings healing to a drought-ridden land.

God promised the Israelites in the wilderness that He would send seasonal rains as a reward for their obedience to Him. The land would produce its crops and the trees would bring forth their fruit. In the times that Israel sinned against Him, God either punished them with torrential storms or withheld the rain.

Like Hosea, who sought a healing shower to revive a rebellious nation, we search for God in our own spiritual droughts. We plead for His forgiveness of our stubborn ways and cling to our hope in Him. We can turn back to the Lord, humble ourselves, and wait expectantly for His cleansing rain to wash away our wickedness. Yes, He loves us that much.

FLOODS

The rain fell, and the floods came, and the winds blew
and slammed against that house; and yet it did not fall,
for it had been founded on the rock.
MATTHEW 7:25 NASB

There's no letup of the downpour, and the water has nowhere to go. We watch the streets fill up, unable to accommodate the flood. Help arrives with sandbags and other supplies to protect our homes and businesses from the rising water. Many times damage is averted as we work together to accomplish a common goal.

We feel helpless when life events pour down on us with no relief in sight. Sometimes it takes a torrent of tears to summon help from others. We can't push back the stress by ourselves, any more than we can stop rushing waters with our bare hands. God places friends, family, and even strangers in our path to help us in our disquieting moments. They come to us bringing the necessary equipment, the wisdom of good advice, and the comfort of outstretched arms.

Our Father provides a strong foundation on which we can rely during our floods: His love shown through others, and His words of truth.

RAINBOW—AN ETERNAL PROMISE

"When the bow is in the cloud, then I will look upon it, to remember the everlasting covenant between God and every living creature of all flesh that is on the earth."

GENESIS 9:16 NASB

Thousands of years have passed since God made His covenant with Noah to never again destroy the earth by flood. And yet, evidence of God's pledge is visible in the cloudy sky on many a rainy day.

A peaceful sense washes over us when we see the familiar multi-colored arch. The rainbow sometimes appears as a continuous span bending from one end of the horizon to the other, or a brief wisp of color in the clouds. We feel twice as blessed to behold a double rainbow.

Photographers and artists try to capture the essence of God's handiwork on film or canvas. But nothing is as brilliant as the original. Their beauty previews what we will see in heaven. The rainbow shimmers like an emerald around God's throne.

When God makes a vow, we can trust Him, even after numerous millennia. His Word is true and His promise is eternal. That is His character.

SOWING IN THE WIND

They sow the wind and they reap the whirlwind.
HOSEA 8:7 NASB

Wind can be gale-force strong or soft as a puff of air, devastating or beneficial. We can't see, grab, or hold it. Yet God commanded the wind to blow back the floodwaters for Noah and part the Red Sea for Moses. When Jesus rebuked the wind, it obeyed Him. In its wildest fury, it remains under God's authority.

God also uses the wind to illustrate the destruction that comes when we are disobedient. The Israelites planted seeds devoid of God's truth in their idolatry. They harvested a crop that yielded emptiness and spewed turmoil like a whirlwind. Not long after that they were taken into captivity.

In our own lives, the temptation to follow other gods is subtle, yet strong. We allow the world to pull us into hero worship when we idolize entertainers, sports figures, and political leaders. They aren't gods, but flawed humans like us.

When the winds of the world blow us toward idolatry, let us turn away. If we sow truth and obedience to the Lord, we will reap calming breezes instead of destructive whirlwinds.

HURRICANES

*The weather changed abruptly, and a wind of typhoon
strength (called a "northeaster") burst across
the island and blew us out to sea.*
ACTS 27:14 NLT

In 2004, Florida acquired the nickname "The Plywood State."
Hurricanes Charlie, Ivan, and Jean targeted the state from three
different directions. After wreaking havoc in Florida's panhandle and
then Alabama, Ivan returned to the East Coast, where it inflicted
even more damage. Before each storm, evacuees clogged the
highways on their way to safety.

A storm and shipwreck sidetracked Paul's journey to Rome.
During his detour on Malta, he illustrated to the islanders God's
protection when he survived a poisonous snakebite. Then he prayed
and healed their leader's ailing father. Other natives then brought
their sick to him for healing.

Although Jesus ordered Paul to Rome to present himself as
a witness, He also gave Paul a three-month delay. The original
destination had to be postponed. The people of Malta needed to
hear about Christ, too.

Evacuated Floridians and tourists took a detour from everyday
life. On the road or staying in a shelter provided opportunities to tell
someone else about Jesus.

In the midst of life's storm, we can look for God's purpose.

POWER OUTAGE

If we walk in the Light as He Himself is in the Light, we have
fellowship with one another, and the blood of Jesus
His Son cleanses us from all sin.
1 JOHN 1:7 NASB

A burst of lightning, a boom of thunder, and suddenly we're in
darkness. We scramble to find a flashlight or matches for a candle.
We fumble around blindly, bumping into furniture or tripping over
objects. Finally, we strike the match or turn on the flashlight and
pierce the darkness.

Like the undetected obstacle that stubs our toe, sin hides in
the shadows waiting for an opportunity to make us fall. But God's
Light is with us to avert that danger. Dark and light cannot occupy
the same space. Even at dusk, a trace of light holds back the night,
if only for a moment.

When we live in submission to God's authority and stay in
fellowship with other believers, He will protect us. With the Lord
at our side, we have no reason to fear the shadows, even on a dark
and stormy night.

A SHELTERED LIFE

It will be a shelter and shade from the heat of the day, and a refuge and hiding place from the storm and the rain.
ISAIAH 4:6 NIV

Shelters serve many purposes. A homeless refuge offers indigents hope by providing a place to rest and a meal. Numerous ministries furnish safe havens for battered and abused women and children. We support organizations to care for our unwanted pets. But nothing compares to the shelter our heavenly Father offers.

Isaiah described one type of shelter God provided for the Israelites. He said that Israel would be protected by a canopy of smoke and clouds, and God's glory would cover them like a blanket.

We need His shelter, too, from the dangers in our world today. Not only from the threats to our personal safety but also from those who would rob us of our joy in Him. There is a devious element that wants us to be too timid to speak about the love of Jesus.

God guides us in the heat of opposition and protects us in the storms of doubt, not with His cloud of glory, but with the shelter of His love.

CLOUD FORMATIONS

"I kept looking in the night visions, and behold, with the clouds of heaven One like a Son of Man was coming, and He came up to the Ancient of Days and was presented before Him."

DANIEL 7:13 NASB

Summer clouds develop into the most fascinating images. The air streams in the upper atmosphere sculpt them with ever-changing currents. They are transformed, moment-by-moment, until a large one with the face of a jolly old man becomes popcorn strewn across the blue sky. Then the smaller clouds come back together and become an angel blowing a trumpet, which might turn into a cat sitting on a pillow.

God used clouds to show His plans for the future to Daniel and His other prophets. He spoke to Moses and Job through them. What does the Lord want us to see when we watch them?

When Jesus ascended to heaven, the angels said He would come again in the same way that He left. One day, we'll see a magnificent cloud coming in the sky. Jesus, the beloved Son of God, will return with great power and glory.

Let's keep looking up!

Discovering God
In Our Work

WORKPLACE HARMONY

"They should always be available to solve the people's common disputes, but have them bring the major cases to you. Let the leaders decide the smaller matters themselves."
EXODUS 18:22–23 NLT

God provided Moses with a wise father-in-law named Jethro, the priest of Midian. This man knew the art of delegating; after all, he had seven daughters. He knew Moses would wear out if he continued counseling the people in their great and small matters. Even the multitude would lose patience as they waited their turn for an answer.

Order in the workplace depends on more than a fair distribution of duties. Harmony thrives when we're in agreement with each other, when we share one goal. We accomplish much when we unite in one purpose. Absolute joy comes to us spontaneously when we put others' needs ahead of our own.

Jesus did that. He viewed us as more important than His own mortal life. In the workplace or anywhere else, harmony can be ours when we mirror Jesus' love.

OUR TRUE BOSS

Whatsoever ye do, do it heartily, as to the Lord and not unto men; knowing that of the Lord ye shall receive the reward of the inheritance; for ye serve the Lord Christ.
COLOSSIANS 3:23–24 KJV

It's easy to forget who our real boss is, especially if we work in a demanding environment. While the person who supervises us and pays our wages deserves our best work, respect, and honesty, we serve the Lord, not a person. He is the One who blesses our employer so that we can receive a salary increase.

That extra income is always helpful, but our reward in heaven is much greater and will last forever. When we're promoted to a higher level and given heavier responsibilities, we can give thanks to our heavenly Father who knows our qualifications.

No matter what our occupation may be, God cares about how we perform. He wants us to do our work wholeheartedly, even when no one is looking.

Let us aim to please the Lord in all we say and do so that others will see God through our work ethic.

DISPUTES IN THE WORKPLACE

You, beloved, building yourselves up on your most holy faith,
praying in the Holy Spirit, keep yourselves in the love of God,
waiting anxiously for the mercy of our Lord Jesus Christ to
eternal life. And have mercy on some, who are doubting.
JUDE 1:20–22 NASB

No matter how hard we try to keep a calm, cool, and composed
mood in our workplace, disagreements will occur. Some arguments
are minor squabbles. Others are nearly earth-shattering conflicts.
The stress of too much work and too little time to complete it also
puts us in a pressure-cooker situation. We're all flawed human
beings, capable of quarrels and hurtful comments.

When disputes occur, let us build up and strengthen our
faith to pray for the right words to calm the tempest of grumblers.
Sometimes that means waiting in silence. Let the love of God
surround us as we show mercy to those who criticize others and us.
Let us also pray for changed hearts—theirs and ours.

God knows the answer. We are His beloved children. He will
guide us to His solution.

IN OFFICE SUPPLIES

Prove all things; hold fast that which is good.
Abstain from all appearance of evil.
1 THESSALONIANS 5:21–22 KJV

Calculators prove our account balances. God established His truth in us through His Word, His Spirit and His Son.

Staples and paper clips hold our documents together. Our faith in the Lord Jesus Christ holds our lives together.

Files keep our documents accessible. God is always accessible to us through prayer.

We organize our thoughts on keyboards. The Holy Spirit inspires us to think and do what is right. We print them on blank paper. Jesus gave us a clean slate. We have a fresh start.

Procedural manuals give us sound instruction. The Bible is the ultimate life manual.

We sign documents with a pen. Our signatures distinguish us from others. God put His permanent mark on us through Jesus, setting us apart from the world.

Correction tape covers our mistakes, making them almost undetectable. Jesus' blood obliterated our sins. God remembers them no more. Glue repairs damaged items. Our heavenly Father has restored what was previously broken.

Organizers help us maintain a professional appearance. The Lord admonishes us to maintain the appearance of good and not evil.

A PROPER EXAMPLE

Make it your goal to live a quiet life, minding your own business
and working with your hands, just as we instructed you before.
1 Thessalonians 4:11 nlt

At His last supper, Jesus poured water into a basin and washed
the disciples' feet. This illustration of humility underscored Christ's
ministry as a servant.

He led a quiet life, not bragging to draw attention to Himself.
He offered to help those who asked, but preferred anonymity.
Neither gossip nor falsehood came from His mouth, nor did He
meddle in others' affairs.

He worked with His hands as a carpenter before His earthly
ministry. Then He used His hands to perform miracles.

His conversation with Nicodemus proved He earned respect
from unbelievers, even though some demanded His life.

Relying solely on His Father in heaven for all provisions, He
asked no favors of anyone. His forgiveness of those who crucified
Him set the standard of His unfathomable love for us.

In setting a good example in our work, let us follow Christ's
model: Grace means service.

IN MEETINGS

The king said to me, "What would you request?"
So I prayed to the God of heaven.
NEHEMIAH 2:4 NASB

As cupbearer to the king, Nehemiah took great care in mulling over his answer. After days of lamenting with a long, penitent prayer over the desolation of Jerusalem, he had unintentionally allowed his sorrow to become obvious. When Artaxerxes questioned him, Nehemiah prayed quickly in silence for the right words. He dared not anger the king.

The Lord God immediately provided the right answer, and Artaxerxes did all that Nehemiah asked, and more.

In our business meetings, we can pray silently as Nehemiah did for the Lord's guidance before offering a suggestion or giving an answer. We can also pray fervently for God's guidance and peace prior to the meeting.

We're not alone when we enter the conference room. The Lord is with us. He will give us the right answers when we seek His counsel. We might not receive the positive results of Nehemiah, but we consulted our King before giving an answer and can trust in His resolution response.

OUR PAYCHECKS

When those hired first came to get their pay, they assumed they would receive more. But they, too, were paid a day's wage.
MATTHEW 20:10 NLT

The landowner's hired hands grumbled at their perceived inequity of salaries, yet they had agreed to work for that wage when they took the job.

In this parable, Jesus doesn't teach the ratio of equal pay for equal work, but illustrates God's boundless mercy. The child who accepts Christ has the same amount of salvation as the older person who professes faith on their deathbed. Salvation is for everyone who'll receive it. No one can be more or less saved than anyone else.

As believers, we're called to be His workmen. Jesus also demonstrates His abundant grace in this parable. God acknowledges our faithfulness according to our various gifts and circumstances. Some are equipped to serve long hours, while others have limitations. We serve the Lord when we can and accept His rewards without question.

We gratefully receive our temporal paychecks as the fruit of our labors for our earthly occupations. Let us rejoice as we store up crowns in heaven with our service to the Lord. God's paycheck is eternal.

WRITING

These things I have written to you who believe in the name of the
Son of God, so that you may know that you have eternal life.
1 JOHN 5:13 NASB

God has provided the means for putting our thoughts in writing. He
opens our minds to offer His sound wisdom. Our hearts pump life
into the words, giving them feelings. Fingers typing on the keyboard
or holding pen to paper give them a purpose. And when we ask in
prayer, He inspires us through His Holy Spirit.

The words the apostle John wrote in his gospel and his epistles
still have two purposes: to tell the world about the love of Jesus
Christ and to help us grow in our faith. Through his writings, he
provides sound testimony that Jesus is the Son of God.

Christian authors write articles, short stories, and books
to share their love for the Lord with the reading world. What a
wonderful opportunity the Lord has given us. In everything we
write, whether a personal letter or a novel, let us share the Good
News of our Savior.

KEYS TO SUCCESS

I will give unto thee the keys of the kingdom of heaven: and whatsoever thou shalt bind on earth shall be bound in heaven: and whatsoever thou shalt loose on earth shall be loosed in heaven.
MATTHEW 16:19 KJV

We use keys to lock doors, gates, or other entryways to keep them secure. Only friends or business associates we trust are allowed access to them. Handing the keys to another means we can depend on their character and good judgment. We expect them to treat the property with the same sense of ownership as we do.

In that same vein, Jesus gave the keys to His kingdom to Simon Peter. These spiritual keys gave him the authority to open the gates to the kingdom to admit believers, and lock them to exclude those who refuse to believe. The apostle proved his faithfulness when he proclaimed, "You are the Christ, the Son of the living God." He didn't hesitate with his answer to the Lord's question, but blurted it out with confidence.

This is the key to success in our faith; we can declare with boldness that Jesus is the Christ, our Savior.

FARMING

"I have made the earth, the men and the beasts which are on the face of the earth by My great power and by My outstretched arm, and I will give it to the one who is pleasing in My sight."
JEREMIAH 27:5 NASB

Roosters crow to bring in the dawn. The farmer is already awake and tending to his chores. His wife fries bacon and eggs in the skillet while coffee brews. But he's in the barn. As a good steward of his livestock, he feeds them before he feeds himself.

Outside, chickens cluck and scratch the ground searching for tidbits. Pigs oink and grunt in their pens. The lowing cattle add their voices to the early morning livestock choir.

The Lord has called him to work the earth, planting crops of vegetables or fruit for food, or cotton for clothing. He gave him knowledge of when to sow, when to harvest, and what to do in between.

As he follows age-old traditions for plowing the ground and caring for his animals, he thanks God for His provisions.

Pleasing in the sight of Almighty God is one who cultivates His soil and watches over His beasts.

HIS SHEEP

My sheep hear my voice, and I know them, and they follow me.
JOHN 10:27 KJV

When my friend's father, James, bought a lamb for his small farm, he didn't bother to choose a name for the animal. He simply called her Sheep.

The first time he took her for shearing, he lost sight of her among the others in the pen. The sheepshearer suggested he call out to her. James admitted she had no name. The sheepshearer grinned and again told him to call her. So James called out, "Hey, Sheep!" His little ewe's head popped up from the midst of all the others and made her way over to him. Sheep may not know their names, but they know their master's voice.

We, too, can recognize our Master's voice. When we sense His prompting, He always points us to the Bible. He will never give us permission to do anything that would harm us or others. And He will always be truthful, for He is the way, the truth, and the life. The Good Shepherd will lead us in the paths of righteousness as we learn to listen for His voice and follow Him.

SPRING CLEANING

Seven days you shall eat unleavened bread, but on the first day you shall remove leaven from your houses; for whoever eats anything leavened from the first day until the seventh day, that person shall be cut off from Israel.

EXODUS 12:15 NASB

We all know what spring cleaning means. That's when we move furniture to expose dust bunnies and retrieve lost coins from the sofa cushions. Everything gets washed, from the floors to the windowsills and beyond.

The Israelite women engaged in spring cleaning as well. But for them it meant searching their homes for leaven in preparation for the Passover Feast. Since it represented sin, they weren't allowed to have even a teaspoon of leaven in their midst.

We can imitate the Israelites' search for leaven by seeking and removing the hidden sin in our lives. Sweep away those alluring temptations. Mop up our spilled good intentions. Launder our minds and let any negative thoughts go down the drain. Polish our silver words of comfort until they gleam. Scrub the windows of our eyes to remove any unwholesome sight. Then put the furniture back in place and take pleasure in a sparkling clean life that delights the Lord.

Discovering God
In Meal Times

THE BEST COOKOUT

At dawn Jesus was standing on the beach, but the disciples couldn't see who he was. He called out, "Fellows, have you caught any fish?"
JOHN 21:4–5 NLT

The third time Jesus manifested Himself to the disciples after His resurrection, He stood on the shore next to a charcoal fire. When He saw that they had been fishing all night but caught no fish, He called out to them, telling them where to cast their nets.

John was the first to recognize Christ, and he remembered the miracle of their massive catch a few years before, so they quickly obeyed. Peter was so glad to see Jesus, though, that he couldn't wait. He dove into the water and swam to Him instead of waiting for the others in the boat. When the others came, Jesus served them breakfast.

We'll share the best cookout in heaven with the Lord, but it won't be hot dogs or burgers with potato salad. Nor will it be fish and bread. We'll feast on unlimited nourishment from the Word of God.

A LITTLE JAR OF OIL

It came to pass, when the vessels were full, that she said unto her
son, Bring me yet a vessel. And he said unto her, There is not a
vessel more. And the oil stayed.
2 Kings 4:6 KJV

We scribble the words *olive oil* on the grocery list when we run low.
Pastas, sauces, and dressings call for it, and we don't want to run
out. The thickness and rich flavor add body to the recipe that other
oils might lack.

Elisha used a small jar of oil to prove God's abundant supply,
and a widow's faith in the Lord. Obedience to the man of God, saved
her from adversity. The widow's sons were in danger of being taken
away from her when she turned to Elisha for help. Not only did the
widow receive all the oil she needed, but there was also enough to
sell and pay her debts.

This simple jar of oil has become a symbol of great faith. God's
provision is as great as our belief and submission to His will.

BAKING FOR SPECIAL OCCASIONS

Gideon hurried home. He cooked a young goat, and with a basket of flour he baked some bread without yeast. Then, carrying the meat in a basket and the broth in a pot, he brought them out and presented them to the angel, who was under the great tree.
JUDGES 6:19 NLT

Homemade bread compliments any meal, and the aroma from the oven whets our appetites. We serve it sliced from a loaf, rolled up as croissants, or cut out as biscuits. If you've ever shared freshly baked bread with a friend or neighbor, you know how enthusiastically it's received.

During the Midianite oppression, Gideon had to secretly thresh out the wheat for fear someone would steal what little he had. Yet he was willing to bake and share it with the stranger who sat under an oak tree nearby. A fiery acceptance of the meal revealed the stranger was the Angel of the Lord.

We bake for family and special friends, and sometimes for strangers as Gideon did. As we offer our tasty gifts from the oven to others, let them see God in our gesture of kindness.

PLANNING A MEAL

Let your speech always be with grace, as though seasoned with salt, so that you will know how you should respond to each person.
COLOSSIANS 4:6 NASB

The spice rack is an essential staple in our kitchens. How bland our food would be without salt, pepper, or a little paprika.

Salt not only flavors our food, but also acts as a preservative. Pepper gives the meal a little punch, depending on how much or how little we use. Paprika and other herbs and spices enhance or change the meal accordingly. We sprinkle oregano on chicken for an Italian flair or give it a light dusting of curry for a hint of Mediterranean cuisine.

Our conversations need a little seasoning, as well. Too much spice will overpower our words, making us appear sharp or offensive. Too little leaves them flavorless and indifferent.

Seasoning our words with kindness keeps us from spoiling our language with tasteless or inappropriate expressions. With a touch of salt, enough to enhance the message, our words will bring grace to the hearer.

MIRACULOUS MEALTIME

*They all did eat, and were filled. And they took up twelve baskets
full of the fragments, and of the fishes. And they that did eat
of the loaves were about five thousand men.*
MARK 6:42–44 KJV

Most everyone has attended a banquet, typically in support of a
cause or ministry. Tables of eight are set with fine china and waiters
serve a salad, an entrée, and a dessert. Afterward, a speaker delivers
an interesting speech, one he or she hopes we'll remember, and the
event is over.

How different a banquet with Jesus must have been. His
guests didn't sit at tables set with fine china, but reclined on a field
of grass in groups of fifty or a hundred. Instead of trained waiters,
Jesus' disciples served the people. The menu consisted of borrowed
bread and fish. The disciples wondered if there would be enough to
feed everyone.

But when the meager provisions were blessed by God's Son,
they fed not only the crowd of more than five thousand, but the
disciples had to pick up leftovers. And our Lord fed them more than
bread and fish; He nourished their souls with words of life.

FRUIT SALAD

The fruit of the Spirit is love, joy, peace, longsuffering,
kindness, goodness, faithfulness, gentleness, self-control.
Against such there is no law.
GALATIANS 5:22–23 NKJV

My fruit salad is different every time I make it. I use whatever I have on hand—fresh strawberries, bananas, kiwi, pineapple, and more.

The fruit of the Spirit, however, always stays the same. Christ's sacrificial love will always be with us. Joy comes when we put Jesus first in our lives. He delivers peace when we are troubled and longsuffering patience when we err. His stretches much further than our own capacity with each other. He teaches us to be kind, good, faithful, and gentle, just as He taught His disciples in the Sermon on the Mount. He also teaches us to turn the other cheek when we are wronged. That takes a great amount of self-control.

I'm glad God makes no changes or substitutions to His fruit salad recipe. It's always delicious and the work it does in our hearts and minds make us worthy to call ourselves His children.

EATING FOR RIGHTEOUSNESS

*The kingdom of God is not eating and drinking, but righteousness
and peace and joy in the Holy Spirit.*
ROMANS 14:17 NKJV

How easy it is to slip off the diet when a sweet roll tempts us,
especially when we think no one is looking. We always check,
though, looking both ways to make sure the coast is clear before
indulging in that high-calorie dessert. We justify it, telling ourselves,
"It's only a little sweet roll." But when we sink our teeth into it,
we're disappointed. It isn't as tasty or fresh as our expectations led
us to believe.

It's just as easy to stagger off the right path when sin lures us
away. We try to justify it. It's only a white lie, or a quick look, or an
innocent flirtation. We think no one will know, but God sees us.

When we take that giant step into the chasm of temptation,
we rob ourselves of God's peace. The experience brings regret
instead of pleasure. The Holy Spirit is here, dwelling within us,
to help turn our focus from physical gratification to the joy of
righteousness. He's as close as a prayer uttered for self-control.

Discovering God In Exercise

POWER WALKING

They set out from the mount of the Lord three days' journey, with the ark of the covenant of the Lord journeying in front of them for three days, to seek out a resting place for them.

NUMBERS 10:33 NASB

Power walking brings unexpected blessings. We find coins on the pavement, meet new friends along the way, and see animal and plant life in action up close. God also gives us expected blessings such as fresh air and sunshine, and a way to burn off a few unwanted calories.

The Israelites did a lot of walking—more than we could imagine. But they had two advantages. They carried God's Law with them in the Ark of the Covenant, and the Lord led them all along the way.

We don't have the Ark to carry, but the Lord is with us in our hearts and minds as we march along the footpath. God prompts us quietly to pray for a person or situation. Or simply to enjoy the peace that comes in being with Him in a natural setting. The secret is to not expect the blessings. It's sweeter when the Lord surprises us.

LEISURELY STROLL

I will walk among you, and will be your God,
and ye shall be my people.
LEVITICUS 26:12 KJV

A leisurely stroll sometimes takes us to surprising destinations. But no matter where we ramble—on the beach, in a mall, or a broad avenue in the city, God walks right along with us.

At the water's edge, we marvel at the intricate design of the shells cast off by creatures that once called them home. A rising and falling fin pulls our attention to the water. Porpoises perform for us, frolicking in the waves. We see God in His creation.

Wandering through a shopping mall, we see a picture in a display window that reminds us of a favorite Bible verse. As we browse in a store, the Lord cues us to share His Good News with the clerk. We see God in His subtle promptings.

On a sidewalk in the city's business district, people brush past us, hurrying to their appointments or meetings. Someone stops in front of us, holding a hand-drawn map, and asks for directions. We offer a quicker, safer route to where they need to go. We see God in small acts of kindness.

REACHING THE GOAL

I run in such a way, as not without aim; I box in such a way,
as not beating the air; but I discipline my body and make
it my slave, so that, after I have preached to others,
I myself will not be disqualified.
1 CORINTHIANS 9:26–27 NASB

We learn the basics of the game first. Then the coach arrives to motivate us to perform at a higher level. Self-discipline becomes the key to reaching our objective. We practice continually, with the coach always pushing us to go beyond our comfort zone. Our goal—the medal, the trophy, or setting a new record—is always in front of us.

Without self-discipline, we stray from the mission. Our focus becomes blurred, and our performance turns sloppy. We're disqualified, and the coach benches us.

As believers in Jesus Christ, our ultimate goal is to spread the Word of Truth. We start with basic training—reading the Bible. God puts the desire to learn more about Him in our hearts. We take notes of sermons and study coursework prepared by biblical scholars. Self-discipline is the key here, as well. Our focus on the Word qualifies us to tell others about our Savior.

RUNNING A MARATHON

*The hand of the LORD was on Elijah, and he girded up
his loins and outran Ahab to Jezreel.*
1 KINGS 18:46 NASB

The runners line up at the starting point, waiting for the signal.
When the signal is given, they're off, following the designated
course. They've trained for months, each day increasing their
stamina, which is the secret to staying in the race.

Our life marathon requires stamina, too, because our race is
against evil. We run with the power to serve the Lord. Isaiah tells us
if we put our hope in the Lord, we will race without getting tired.
God gives us strength and endurance to withstand any opposition.

We also need to run with enthusiasm as we serve the Lord.
Peter and John both rushed to the tomb when they heard the stone
had been rolled away. God gives us the zeal to proclaim our faith.

We must run with the purpose, too. Paul tells us to perform in
such a way as to claim the prize.

God granted Elijah the power to outdistance a chariot. He will
give us the stamina, enthusiasm, and purpose we need to finish our
race as well.

Discovering God In Our Natural Environment

BUTTERFLIES ARE FREE

When we are young, it is good to struggle hard and to sit silently alone, if this is what the LORD intends.
LAMENTATIONS 3:27-28 CEV

The butterfly pushes against a wall of woven silk, struggling to escape his cocoon. We pity the insect as we watch him strive to be free. But he needs that exertion to develop his beautiful and powerful wings.

Sometimes God intends for us to have difficulties in our lives. We push with all our might against a barrier, not realizing how much stronger we have become. The experience fortifies us to face the obstacles. We learn patience and perseverance, and to trust in Him. Instead of asking why we must endure this trial, we can sit silently alone and pray, confident that God will use our new strength for His purposes.

The butterfly doesn't realize the effort to break out of the cocoon will allow him the pleasure of flying long distances to visit beautiful flowers. What exciting adventure is God preparing for us? Our efforts for God are never wasted.

DROPPING SEEDS

Neither the one who plants nor the one who waters is anything,
but only God, who makes things grow.
1 Corinthians 3:7 NIV

A squirrel tucks an acorn into his mouth and searches for a hiding place. He digs a hole, drops the nutritional nugget in the ground, and covers it with dirt. He has unwittingly planted a would-be oak. He won't return to water it and watch it grow. His intention is to store it for food. He might forget where he buried it, but God knows where it is.

God uses the efforts of this small creature to produce another mighty oak that will drop many more acorns. Some of them destined to mature, while others provide food for the industrious squirrel. God's perfect cycle propagates the forests and rewards His creatures for their part in His design.

In a similar cycle, our heavenly Father knows where we drop seeds of the Gospel. He sends others behind us to water them, perpetuating His message. He rewards us with blessings in our endeavors to spread the Gospel to the lost.

FLIGHT SCHOOL

I will instruct you and teach you in the way you should go;
I will counsel you with my loving eye on you.
PSALM 32:8 NIV

The starlings nesting in a tree use specific whistles and chirps to
teach their babies to fly. It's fascinating to watch, as the youngsters
listen to and obey their parents' instructions. Their sounds resemble
a song rather than flight training. But if we want to understand
them, we'll need a translator.

The Bible seems like disconnected stories to the unbeliever.
The Holy Spirit translates God's messages to us when we believe in
the Lord Jesus Christ. In it, we follow history from creation to the
crucifixion. The generations listed in Genesis are recorded again in
Luke, recounting the lineage of Jesus—through Mary—back to Adam.

The record of the multiple times the Israelites spurned God,
then returned to His waiting arms of forgiveness give us hope. He
continued to send them prophets to teach them His ways.

The Lord gives us life instructions through His Word. Like the
baby starlings being taught to fly, we learn by listening to and
obeying the Lord's signals.

FALL FROM THE NEST

Restore us to You, O Lord, that we may be restored.
LAMENTATIONS 5:21 NASB

An indoor cat paws hungrily at the window. Birds chirp and swoop toward the ground near the oak tree in the front yard. A baby bird has fallen out of his nest. Frightened and disoriented, he manages to climb up the tree, fluttering his inept little wings all the way. He makes it back to his safe haven unscathed, restored to his family.

The little bird may have fallen because he was looking at the world around him instead of being content inside the nest.

The Israelites were taken into captivity over and over again because of their unfaithfulness to God. They became enamored with the world outside and left God's protective nest. Yet each time they returned to worship Him, He restored them to their safe haven—the land of promise.

Keeping our eyes focused on Jesus instead of the world prevents us from falling out of the nest. And in those times when we do, He will help us climb back to safety and restore us to His family.

SOARING HUMILITY

*Though you seem to soar like an eagle and make your
nest among the stars, even from there I will bring you down.
This is the Lord's declaration.*

OBADIAH 1:4 HCSB

Eagles build their nests on high cliffs, telephone poles, even on top
of city skyscrapers. They're visible to us, but inaccessible from the
ground.

The eagle might appear arrogant when he thrusts out his
chest and flashes his haughty eyes. He looks down at us from his
aerie, knowing we pose no threat to him or his offspring. But God is
higher than his lofty home.

The bird soars above us, spotting his food source below with
near-perfect vision. His strong talons capture his prey. But God
provides his meal. In all his strength and abilities, he, too, must rely
on his Creator.

Like eagles, the Edomites built their homes in lofty places,
high in the cliffs of Petra. Their pride led them to believe they were
invincible. God allowed them to be destroyed because of their
arrogance. Not one of Esau's descendents survived the coming
battle described by the prophet Obadiah. Pride drags us down, but
humility lets us soar.

MORNING STAR

*We have the prophetic word made more sure, to which you do well
to pay attention as to a lamp shining in a dark place, until the day
dawns and the morning star arises in your hearts.*

2 PETER 1:19 NASB

I slipped outside, bleary-eyed, in the pre-dawn hours to get the
newspaper. I blinked a couple of times to clear my vision and stood
in awe of a bright star low in the eastern sky. It shone down on the
sleeping city as though announcing the coming of dawn. A faint
gray light blushed at the horizon. The beauty of the scene took my
breath away. Had I not been paying attention, I might have missed
the morning star rising before the dawn.

Our heavenly Father has planted subtle hints concerning the
fulfillment of His Scripture. He set the planet Venus in the sky to
be the portent of the true Morning Star to come—Jesus. We live in
a dark world. Our light of hope is God's Word, which guides us like
a lamp lighting our steps. If we pay attention, we won't miss the
Morning Star rising in our hearts on the day of His return.

THE LIGHT OF DAWN

The path of the righteous is like the light of dawn, that shines brighter and brighter until the full day.

PROVERBS 4:18 NASB

When we stray from the Lord, we often find ourselves groping in the darkness, desperately searching for Him. We fumble blindly, weighed down in our despair. Then a tiny speck of light appears on the horizon. It grows brighter and brighter, beckoning us to leave the darkness behind. It is the righteous path, available to any who want to follow the Lord.

The first step is the hardest, and taken by faith. Where do we put our foot? The next one gets us closer. The one after that brings us nearer to the light. The whole path is now glowing with the brightness of His love, leading us straight into our Savior's outstretched arms.

We have no reason to look back. The darkness behind us turns gray before it vanishes in the brilliance before us. He bathes us in His righteousness, washing away our doubts and fears. Then He whispers, "Welcome home, My child."

HIGH NOON

The sun stopped in the middle of the sky and delayed its setting almost a full day.
JOSHUA 10:13 HCSB

Midway through our day, we look back at the morning with a smile. The early morning shadows have fled. We can now anticipate the transition to afternoon. God grants us the gift of the noon hour. The world looks bright and fresh in the sunlight.

But when lunchtime ends, the afternoon's shadowed fingers reach out with their demands of do this, go there, pick up, check on—a myriad of busyness. If only we could ask the Lord to hold back the sun like He did for Joshua. We could savor this hour a bit longer before returning to work.

Instead we remember that time is a gift from God. With each checked-off item on our "to do" list, we give thanks for the moments we have to accomplish these daily goals. Our sense of purpose is satisfied when our tasks are pleasing to the Lord. We who dwell in the shelter of the Most High will abide in the shadow of the Almighty.

SOLAR ECLIPSE

*It shall come to pass in that day, saith the Lord God,
that I will cause the sun to go down at noon, and I will
darken the earth in the clear day.*
Amos 8:9 KJV

In Amos' day, a total eclipse of the sun foretold coming judgment.
Today, we watch these stunning displays as a curious phenomenon.
But perhaps there's another meaning?

The moon can't produce light; it only reflects it. In a similar
way, Satan can only replicate the lights, signs, and wonders God
created.

In a solar eclipse, the moon overshadows the sun. The
adversary's sole desire is to extinguish God's light with his darkness.
He thought he had snuffed out the Light when Jesus died on the
cross. But just as the sun emerges from the corner of an eclipse,
Jesus rose from the dead. He pushed the darkness back and came
forward from the other side.

When it seems darkness might triumph in our lives, let us
remember the solar eclipse lasts only a short time. God's light will
return more glorious than before. The sun is greater than the moon.
And the Son is greater than a fallen angel.

SHOUT JOYFULLY, O SUNSET

They who dwell in the ends of the earth stand in awe of Your signs;
You make the dawn and the sunset shout for joy.
PSALM 65:8 NASB

The afternoon sun begins its retreat, sinking closer and closer to the horizon. Light filters through the angles of the upper atmosphere, drawing pink and violet across the blue of the western sky. Sunbeams skim across the high clouds and cut through the lower atmosphere. They invite the dazzling orange with wide strokes of deep crimson and mauve to join the heavenly choir of colors. Each hue carries its own musical tone.

Every sunset is different. Some show soft purples or pinks with a blush of pale orange. Others blaze fiery red encircled by a golden halo. Heavy clouds might obscure others. But the sun's rays find a way to burst forth through them or from behind them, shining in pure white bands or an explosion of colors.

Whether a sunset is dramatically brilliant or peacefully subdued, it sings out the glory of God's name. Shout joyfully to God all the earth.

MOON AND STARS

God is more glorious than the moon;
he shines brighter than the stars.
JOB 25:5 NLT

We marvel at a super-moon, when the full moon comes closest to the earth in its elliptical orbit. It bathes the countryside in white light. We could almost read a book standing in a field at midnight. But God is more glorious than a super-moon. He is the Light; not a reflection.

The weatherman reports an impending meteor shower in the wee hours of the morning. We'll stumble out of bed at three o'clock, put on our robes, and step outside to watch the heavenly performance. For a few minutes bright lights zip across the sky, leaving bluish-green streaks. But God is more glorious than a meteor shower. He is eternal, not a momentary light show.

The stars sparkle like diamonds in the night sky. Sometimes they seem so close that we could reach out and touch them. Yet they are indeed far away. But God outshines the stars. He is always within reach; not in a distant, inaccessible galaxy, but here with us.

Our life-giving, eternal, approachable Lord; how glorious is His name.

CONSTELLATIONS

*Who makes the Bear, Orion and the Pleiades,
and the chambers of the south?*
JOB 9:9 NASB

The stars that form the constellations have remained in their
assigned places since the day they were created. God placed them in
the sky as a glorious declaration of His plan for mankind. He knew
before He created them that Adam and Eve would sin, bringing
Eden, their beautiful home, down with them.

Job saw Ursa Major, Orion, and the Pleiades and counted
himself worthless in comparison. David rejoiced in the stars,
realizing that in all their vastness, God valued man more. Amos and
Isaiah saw them and predicted the coming judgment of those who
would be unfaithful to the Lord. The magi studied the constellations
and journeyed to Jerusalem to search for the King.

Now we behold them.

As the heavens proclaim the glory of God, we recognize the
shapes and patterns specific to a constellation and find hope in the
prophecy spread across the sky. It tells of the Redeemer who came
and suffered, but will return to crush the head of the tempter. God
loves us so much; He reaches out to us even through the stars.

THE MORNING DEW

When the dew fell upon the camp in the night,
the manna fell upon it.
NUMBERS 11:9 KJV

The Israelites in the wilderness yearned for the bread they ate in Egypt. How quickly they forgot the brutal taskmasters and hardships they'd left behind. They looked back when they faced challenges, disregarding the miracles God performed through Moses on their long trek through the wilderness.

But God never failed to provide for them. First came the life-giving water as dew; followed by the sustaining bread of heaven as manna. The Lord supplied this wafer-like food to nourish them each morning. It was a foretelling of the Savior who would come as the bread of life to feed us, not for a day, but for eternity.

Manna doesn't fall upon our dew today because Jesus, the manifestation of God in the flesh, the living, breathing bread of life, has already come. We let the morning dew soak into the earth and nourish the grass, while we gather our manna every day by reading His Word.

RIVERS

On the last day, the great day of the feast, Jesus stood and cried out, saying, "If anyone is thirsty, let him come to Me and drink. He who believes in Me, as the Scripture said, 'From his innermost being will flow rivers of living water.'"
JOHN 7:37–38 NASB

Whether we are traveling east or west, we cannot span the width of this beautiful nation we call America without crossing the legendary Mississippi River. This peaceful waterway flows south from its source at Lake Itasca in Minnesota and ends at the Gulf of Mexico. At no time in recorded history has it run dry.

God created the cycle that feeds the tributaries with a continual flow of water. Winter brings snow and ice. Spring comes with its warmth to melt it, allowing streams to flow into the lake. The lake supplies the river, and so the cycle continues. But one day these lakes and rivers will run dry.

The River of Life that Jesus offers us has no beginning or end. It doesn't rely on cyclical weather, but flows as the Holy Spirit from within Him. We who have tasted His crystal clear water will never thirst.

PICKING UP ROCKS AND STONES

"The Rock! His work is perfect. For all His ways are just; a God of faithfulness and without injustice, righteous and upright is He."
DEUTERONOMY 32:4 NASB

Rocks and stones lie on the ground, lifeless and insignificant. But God sculpted each one. He commanded Moses to strike one to provide water for the Israelites in the Sinai. A generation later in the wilderness of Zin, God told Moses and Aaron to speak to the rock and tell it to spew water.

Moses and David sang songs to praise the Lord. They proclaimed Him as the Rock of their salvation, a fortress and shield, deliverer and the foundation of their faith.

Jesus declared Peter's strong faith as the rock on which He would build His church. And when the Pharisees told Jesus to rebuke His disciples, He replied that if He could silence them, then even the stones would cry out. And one stone did cry out, although not verbally. But it must have rejoiced as it shattered the Roman seals and rolled away from Jesus' tomb to prove He had risen.

God is indeed our Rock, righteous and just. And perfect.

MUSIC OF THE FOREST

Then shall the trees of the wood sing out at the presence of the
LORD, because he cometh to judge the earth. O give thanks unto the
LORD; for he is good; for his mercy endureth for ever.
1 CHRONICLES 16:33–34 KJV

King David rejoiced with the elders of Israel when they brought back
the Ark of the Covenant. As he sang his praises, others joined in,
playing their instruments. He imagined even the trees of the forest
singing for joy.

Today, when we walk through a forest, let us take in the sweet
sounds King David envisioned. The Concertmaster raises His baton.
His creation obeys, preparing to perform in His orchestra. He directs
the wind to blow through the trees. Their trunks sigh in mellow
tones as they sway back and forth. The leaves whisper through
waving branches.

The woodpecker joins in as percussion with his drumbeat on
a tree's bark. Small birds chirp and tweet their melodious song.
Squirrels scamper through the treetops, and chipmunks scurry along
the forest floor, chattering the notes of the scale.

No orchestra can compete with the music of the forest. Praise
the LORD for His woodland symphony.

LOGS

You can see the speck in your friend's eye.
But you don't notice the log in your own eye.
LUKE 6:41 CEV

I put a log on the dwindling flame, scattering ashes and embers in the fireplace. A cinder flew up into my eye, causing it to fill with tears. In a matter of minutes, I had a bloodshot roadmap across my eyeball. The particle and tears also blurred my vision. After removing the speck and blotting the cleansing tears, I watched that smoldering log and considered Jesus' message. It's nearly impossible to ignore even a tiny cinder in one of our eyes, and yet, we often choose instead to concern ourselves with what is in the eye of another.

I've observed we are most critical of flaws in others that mirror our own. Pride can keep us from believing that we are not as desperately in need of cleansing and forgiveness as those around us.

Let us be quick to cleanse our own eyes. Only then can we help others remove those things that keep them from seeing the truth God has placed before them and further, rather than hinder, His purposes.

Discovering God In Gardening

GRAFTING TREES

Do not be arrogant toward the branches; but if you
are arrogant, remember that it is not you who
supports the root, but the root supports you.
ROMANS 11:18 NASB

When grafting a wild olive tree into a cultivated one, the strong roots of one is joined with the fruitfulness of another. The wild tree might produce small olives, but inhibits pests and disease. The other might have a frail root system, but yields larger fruit. Grafting combines the best traits.

God set up this principle from the beginning, knowing He would graft Gentile believers into His divine olive tree. We all need the combined traits of both faith and obedience to be fruitful servants for Him. But the apostle Paul cautions us about arrogance in our position. Being joined by new birth offers a place of privilege in His kingdom, but we must not snub the cultivated branches God will restore one day.

His promised blessing of redemption through Christ is the sturdy root that supports our branches. Remembering His sacrifice on the cross restores our humility.

BLOOMING BROMELIADS

*There appeared to them tongues as of fire distributing themselves,
and they rested on each one of them.*
ACTS 2:3 NASB

Pentecost is one of the four annual feasts the Lord ordained for the Israelites. This particular day of Pentecost, after the ascension of Jesus, fulfilled what the prophet Joel had foretold: that God would pour forth His Spirit on mankind. This miracle used the image of tongues of fire that descended on Christ's followers, causing many to believe in Him.

When the fiery red blooms of mature bromeliads explode out of their green chutes, they resemble flaming tongues. The spiked flowers sometimes last for months before they fade and die. When the flower dies, the plant also dies. But before dying, the mother plant sends out smaller pups to continue the production of flowers.

Like the flaming red bromeliads, which leave descendants in the garden before their death, the legacy of Christ's followers with their tongues of fire, lives on in the Bible. This showy flower brings to mind the miracle of the Holy Spirit's power.

FIELDS OF FLOWER GARDENS

We are both God's workers. And you are God's field.
You are God's building.
1 CORINTHIANS 3:9 NLT

Wildflowers flourish without assistance. God's invisible attributes, unending power, and divine nature produce a field of multicolored blossoms. A cultivated garden, with its proper edging and color-coordinated flowers arranged in specific patterns, also shows God's perfect order. Both proclaim His glory.

We spread the Gospel in the same way wildflowers sow their seeds. A bird carries the seed and drops it in the soil. A breeze blows the dirt over the seed. The rain comes to water it. But God causes it to germinate.

In a similar way, we cultivate a flower garden by carrying seeds to the soil, digging a hole, and then covering the seed with dirt. We dampen the soil with water and again, its growth depends on God.

As tillers of God's garden, one of us may plant when we evangelize, and another may water when we teach, but only God enables the seeds of faith to develop.

NIGHT BLOOMING CACTUS

He was transfigured before them; and His garments became radiant and exceedingly white, as no launderer on earth can whiten them.
MARK 9:2–3 NASB

The pure-white cactus flower blooms only at night. Those fortunate enough to witness its inner light glowing in the dark are always surprised by its beauty. The flower closes before dawn, hiding its brilliant splendor from the daytime world. Would anyone appreciate its loveliness as much in the harsh sun?

Of all the disciples, only Peter, James, and John witnessed the transformation of Jesus from their humble teacher into the radiant Son of God on the mountaintop. As He met with Moses and Elijah, the three disciples caught a glimpse into the future of Jesus' imminent glory and His coming kingdom.

After this miraculous event, Jesus ordered them not to reveal to anyone what they had seen. He had to keep His brilliant splendor a secret from the world. No one would understand or appreciate His glory until He had defeated death.

In the same way the cactus flower withholds its splendor only for the night, Jesus concealed His glory for just the right time.

ARTIFICIAL FLOWERS

You have been born again, not of perishable seed, but of
imperishable, through the living and enduring word of God.
1 PETER 1:23 NIV

Artificial flowers don't wilt and die like natural plants. They need
no water or pesticides to maintain their beauty. We consider them
imperishable because of their long-lasting appearance. But over
time, plastic roses lose their flexibility and crumble into brittle
pieces. Silk daisies unravel. A tissue paper carnation held together
with a hairpin will disintegrate. These imitations lack the soft petals
and sweet fragrance of live flowers. They are simply replicas.

We were like artificial flowers before we believed in Christ.
We appeared to be alive, but inside we were dead in our sins.
Our inflexibility to change caused us to crumble within. Smooth,
silky goals we made for our future unraveled, and our perishable
moments in time disintegrated like paper. We lacked the softness
and gentle scent of one who walks with the Lord.

Being born again through God's living and enduring Word
changed us from silk daisies into living violets that will never wilt.
He has made us imperishable. We will bloom forever.

CLINGING VINES

Beloved, do not imitate what is evil, but what is good. The one who does good is of God; the one who does evil has not seen God.
3 JOHN 11 NASB

I planted two ivies on either side of an arched trellis in my backyard. Each plant sent vines creeping up the lattice. They met at the top, overlapped each other, and then crept down the other side. The trellis, no longer visible, is now an ivy-covered archway.

Clinging vines like ivy take the shape of the object they cover, such as an arbor or a wall. By nature they conform to that image. They have no choice.

As beloved children of the Most High God, His character is our pattern to imitate. The enemy entices us to take the form of the worldly "everyone does it" mind-set. But as we immerse ourselves in the water of His words, we grow in knowledge, and our renewed desires bend us into the shape of righteousness. Holding fast to sound teaching, we reach up over the trellis of Truth and conform to His goodness.

A WEED'S TESTIMONY OF HOPE

What strength do I have that I should continue to hope?
What is my future, that I should be patient?
JOB 6:11 HCSB

The rough, discouraging day finally ended. As I merged onto the local expressway, I caught a glimpse of a weed growing through the asphalt and stretching toward the sky. Could a weed be stronger than asphalt? And why would it be growing where cars would run over it?

Surely God gave me that moment as a testimony of hope. Life has boundless forms of highways and cars—issues which hinder our growth toward God. But unlike the little weed, God gave us freedom of choice. When life tries to pave over us, we can either let trouble win or reach toward God. We can tremble when life's menacing cars run us over, or look to our Lord for hope.

As surely as the inner strength He placed in a little weed can split asphalt, God will embolden us to keep growing up toward Him, regardless of any adverse circumstances we might face.

Discovering God In Reflections And Light

MIRRORS

All of us who have had that veil removed can see and reflect the glory of the Lord. And the Lord—who is the Spirit—makes us more and more like him as we are changed into his glorious image.
2 CORINTHIANS 3:18 NLT

A mirror reflecting into another mirror perpetually echoes the image into infinity. But covering one mirror with a veil disrupts the link, blocking the duplication of the image.

In this letter to the Corinthians, the apostle Paul mentions the veil Moses wore in the presence of the Israelites. After meeting with Almighty God on Mount Sinai or in the Tent of Meeting his face radiated with the light of God's glory. Moses' gleaming countenance so frightened them that he had to cover it with a veil. He gave them the law, which exposed the hopeless stain of man's sinful nature.

As Christians, we mirror God's love, which offers redemption for man's sinful nature. Even when our godly lifestyle and righteous words and deeds make unbelievers uncomfortable, we cannot cover them. Like reflecting mirrors, we want the image of the glory of the Lord to shine brightly through us.

OPENING WINDOWS

Though I sit in darkness, the LORD will be my light.
MICAH 7:8 NLT

During World War II, the British people covered their windows with blackout curtains. They dared not let the enemy see a crack of light in any windows or doors. A sense of danger loomed over them with the dread of another bombing attack.

Sometimes we sit in darkness and hide in the shadows. We draw the drapes over our hearts like a shroud. Why do we linger there? Are we fearful, as the British in the 1940s were, that the enemy will see our light? Do we seek refuge from spiritual or emotional attacks?

The prophet Micah sat in the darkness, waiting patiently for God's mercy. He knew in the midst of his distress that the Lord of Hosts would be his light.

The British no longer cover their windows with blackout curtains. The war is over; the battle has been won. With the Lord's help, we can push aside the oppressive curtains of our sorrow and throw open the windows to let in His light. The spiritual war is over, and the victory belongs to the Lord God Almighty.

USING A FLASHLIGHT

Jesus said to them, "For a little while longer the Light is among you. Walk while you have the Light, so that darkness will not overtake you; he who walks in the darkness does not know where he goes."
JOHN 12:35 NASB

My husband and I carry a flashlight during our evening walks. It illuminates our route and makes drivers aware of our presence on the road. Although the streetlights help, mature trees in our neighborhood cast shadows on our paths.

The Lord Jesus Christ admonished the people He taught to walk in His light while He was still among them. As He prepared for the cross, He warned them not to revert to their previous way of life.

Our enemy, the Devil, wants the darkness to overtake us. If we stay in the shadowy gloom and fail to allow God's Word to show us the way, we won't see the sin lurking in our path. But with God's guidance, we can sidestep evil.

With His light in us, we will shine, making others aware of His presence. And we'll know we're on the right path.

Discovering God at the Seashore

WATCHING THE WAVES

He must ask in faith without any doubting, for the one who doubts
is like the surf of the sea, driven and tossed by the wind.
JAMES 1:6 NASB

The ebb and flow of the sea is predictable, but not fixed. The shoreline moves up and down on the beach with the tide. Those who fluctuate in their faith are like the waves crashing in on the beach then retreating as quickly as they came. Their exit lacks the zeal of their entrance. They appear confident at first, but haven't the wisdom to trust in Jesus, especially during difficult times. They shrink back when doubt tosses them about.

When we ask God for wisdom, we prove our faithfulness to Him by submitting to His will. We can trust Him to grant what we ask with amazing abundance. For wisdom comes from more than memorized verses and church membership. It comes from a reverent relationship with the Most High God.

As we watch the waves roll in to the shore, we know we can trust in the stability of God's wisdom. Whether in difficulties or comfort, all we have to do is ask Him.

CHASING SANDPIPERS

*If we truly love others and live as Christ did in this world, we won't
be worried about the day of judgment. A real love for others will
chase those worries away.*

1 JOHN 4:17–18 CEV

I enjoy watching sandpipers run along the water's edge, scooping
up coquinas to eat from the wet sand. The surf rolls in and chases
the little birds beyond the water's reach. Then, as the wave recedes,
they dash back to gobble down more coquinas.

Our concerns for the future might run along the shorelines of
our minds, feeding on our doubts or fears. But, like the power of the
surf, our trust in the Lord will chase those anxieties away. We love
each other because of our Father's great love for us. His love abides
in us the moment we believe in Christ.

We will be able to approach the judgment seat in the next life
with confidence because we lived out Christ's love in this life.

As the sandpipers run the length of the shoreline, let us
consider the doubts the enemy wants us to have. We can boldly
chase away those fears with a tidal wave of love for one another.

HIDDEN DANGER

We are not fighting against flesh-and-blood enemies,
but against evil rulers and authorities of the unseen world,
against mighty powers in this dark world, and against
evil spirits in the heavenly places.
EPHESIANS 6:12 NLT

One the most vividly painful memories from my youth is a jellyfish sting. While swimming in the Gulf of Mexico, its tentacles lashed across my back like a whip. Multiple welts burned into my skin and my mind. To this day, I won't swim in the Gulf in August, when jellyfish lurk underwater.

Satan's demons conceal themselves to strike at us unaware. Their flaming arrows of temptation strike to discredit our Christian testimonies. Since they can't have our souls, which belong to the Lord, they try to neutralize us.

The Lord of Hosts provides our armor for protection against Satan's attacks. We put on truth, righteousness, the Gospel, our faith, salvation, and His Word. And He will send His angels to guard us in all our ways.

RIDING A RIPTIDE

Behold, you are trusting in deceptive words to no avail.
JEREMIAH 7:8 NASB

We swim in an ocean or a calm river for recreation, often giving no thought to the possibility of a strong underlying riptide that can come upon a swimmer without warning. Like a surge, it drags them along a swift undercurrent. Efforts to break away prove futile, except when experienced swimmers know how to ride the riptide. Most of these areas have signs posted to warn swimmers of the dangers.

Jeremiah warned the people of Jerusalem about God's coming wrath for their plummet into false religion. But they took Jerusalem's past deliverance for granted and ignored the prophet's warnings. They continued breaking God's commandments.

Deceptive words creep into our worship experience with gentle subtlety at first. Then, without warning, they grip us and drag us deeper into the whirlpool of false teaching. God has provided words of warning for us in the Bible. If we heed them, we'll avoid being pulled along the swift undercurrent into a riptide of spurious beliefs. He delivers us from evil.

Discovering God
In Our Fellowship

BEST FRIENDS FOREVER

The LORD be between me and thee,
and between my seed and thy seed for ever.
1 SAMUEL 20:42 KJV

The bond we share with a best friend is as thick as wet cement, and just as solid when it dries. We share common interests, beliefs, and values. Revealing our innermost fears and desires, we are confident our secrets will be treated as classified information and not used to judge us.

Proximity isn't an issue. Our friendship endures great distances and spans generations. Best friends stand together in troubling times. We defend each other's honor, soothe broken hearts, and lift needs—great or small—to God in prayer. Best friends are willing to sacrifice, even unto death to protect us.

Our Lord Jesus Christ models perfect friendship. We can share our deepest secrets with Him without fear of judgment. He stands by us in plenty and in want. He protects us from evil, calms our despair, and advocates our needs to the Father. His love for us extends beyond this world into eternity. And He died to save us from God's wrath for our sinful nature. He truly is our Best Friend Forever.

THE LONG-DISTANCE MOVE

Abram was seventy-five years old when the Lord told him
to leave the city of Haran. He obeyed and left with his wife Sarai,
his nephew Lot, and all the possessions and slaves
they had gotten while in Haran.
GENESIS 12:4–5 CEV

Mixed emotions rose within us when our pastor left the little
church where we worshipped. We would miss his excellent Bible
teaching, but celebrated the honor of his call to the mission field.
Tears of sadness blended with tears of joy as he packed up his wife
and three children and headed for Brazil.

Abram didn't travel as far when he left his relatives in the
city of Haran. While the pastor's destination was clear before he
ventured out, Abram only knew what direction to take. But both
brave men answered God's call without question.

Our pastor's mission, we later learned, was to clean out a snake
pit of corruption in a small town in Brazil. After a successful year,
with Brazilian heads reeling, the pastor and his family returned, but
not to the church. Other mission work beckoned him.

From Brazil to Ukraine and beyond, the Lord blesses this pastor
for his faithful obedience.

PRAYING FOR EACH OTHER

This is the confidence which we have before Him, that, if we ask anything according to His will, He hears us.
1 JOHN 5:14 NASB

When we pray for friends or family members, we may not see the connective issues. Our heavenly Father views the circumstances through omniscient eyes. Praying in God's will implies yielding our own. He might allow a tragic event to unite family members. Does He want us to share our faith with someone close to the situation?

In a hospital, we might witness a miraculous healing or comfort a loved one on their peaceful transition to heaven. Sometimes a physical ailment brings about a spiritual healing. Each prayer can transform us into God's vessels. A stranger who sees us on our knees calling upon the Lord might be moved to inquire about our faith.

The Lord's reply might take us on a journey we hadn't planned. When we look back on previous prayers, we see the route He mapped out for our lives. Opening ourselves to His will reveals the bigger picture. We can confidently accept God's answer with grateful hearts.

ACROSS THE MILES

I long to see you again.
2 TIMOTHY 1:4 NLT

I left friends and family behind when I moved out of state. It was the loneliest five years of my life. I felt cut off from the rest of the world as I started a new job in a place far from my comfort zone.

My father's voice brought joy when he'd call. I relived fun times through cards and letters from folks back home. Keeping those connections across the miles eased my homesick heart.

Paul must have felt isolated, too, while imprisoned in Rome. But his letters to Timothy relate his hope of seeing him again. He expressed joy despite his gloomy dungeon surroundings. Although he longed to see Timothy, his imprisonment barred any possibility of a reunion with his young disciple in Christ. They're together now in heaven.

Continuing our distant friendships preserves the root of belonging to each other. While miles and circumstances keep us apart physically, we can look forward to a hope-filled reunion, if not here, then in heaven with Christ. With the thread of His divine love, God has woven together an indestructible bond that endures across the miles.

FAIR-WEATHER FRIENDS

The men that were at peace with thee have deceived thee, and
prevailed against thee; they that eat thy bread
have laid a wound under thee.
OBADIAH 1:7 KJV

Learning to trust again after a friend's betrayal is a long, arduous journey. Doubts build up within the heart, casting suspicion on the intentions of our true friends. We blame ourselves, convinced we should have seen signs of the approaching back stab. Our self-worth plummets as the feeling of being thrown away sinks into our minds. Healing from this emotional wound feels like climbing out of a tar pit of sadness.

God allowed the betrayal of the Edomites in Obadiah's account because of their haughty delight over Jerusalem's devastation. Since we have the salvation of the Lord, the breach of trust we experience is not punishment. It stands as a test of our capacity to forgive.

Jesus forgave Judas for handing Him over to the enemy. He forgives us when we are disloyal and spurn His love. And He is willing to help us when we need to forgive others. People can be fickle, but we know the Lord is always faithful.

DINING WITH FRIENDS

*When they were hungry, you sent bread from heaven, and when
they were thirsty, you let water flow from a rock.*
NEHEMIAH 9:15 CEV

Progressive dinners take the pressure off one host and spread it
evenly among all the participants. To include our friends who live
farther away, we delegate several people to each course. They plan
their dish as a group. The event begins with the first household
serving *hors d'oeuvres.* Then the guests move to the second house
for salad, then to the third for the main course, and the fourth for
dessert and coffee.

Our caravan from house to house doesn't quite resemble the
Israelites wandering in the wilderness after their exodus from Egypt.
The food doesn't fall from heaven and our beverages don't flow
from a rock, but God still provides our meal. We offer our prayer of
thanks, asking God to bless each course. The dessert and coffee time
ends with a prayer to keep us safe as we make our way back home.

We begin and end this sweet fellowship in the presence of our
Lord, the giver of the feast.

THE GOOD CHINA

If you keep yourself pure, you will be a special utensil
for honorable use. Your life will be clean, and you will be ready
for the Master to use you for every good work.
2 Timothy 2:21 NLT

Everyday dishes serve us well at regular meals, but special guests and holidays require our fine china, the best dishes in the house. The matching dinner plates, salad bowls, and cups and saucers present an elegant display. The dishes seem to sparkle from their place settings in the flickering candlelight.

Whether we inherit these fine pieces of tableware from earlier generations or receive them as gifts, we treat them with special care. When washing them, we handle them gently to avoid breakage.

We are like fine china to the Lord Jesus Christ. He has washed away the crumbs of our sinful nature with His sacrificial love and handles us with tender care. No matter how we came to Him, He treasures us as precious vessels. We honor Him through our faithful service to others. In our obedience to His Word, He uses us for His highest purposes.

LAUGHING OUT LOUD

Sarah said, "God has made laughter for me;
everyone who hears will laugh with me."
GENESIS 21:6 NASB

Sarah laughed to herself, possibly in doubt, when the Lord told
her she would bear a son. We justify her skepticism in our human
viewpoint. She had not conceived a child in her younger years, how
could she possibly become pregnant in her old age? But nothing
is impossible with God. A year later, she laughed out loud with joy
when she gave birth to her son, Isaac.

God created us with the ability to laugh, to find humor in
situations—and in ourselves. Whether we chuckle when we're in
doubt or giggle at an amusing anecdote, we need to laugh.

Good hearty laughter is medicine for our souls. It brightens
our frame of mind, releases healing endorphins to cheer us up, and
spreads our joy to those around us. Almost as contagious as a flu
virus, even strangers will laugh with us, often unaware of what
tickled our funny bones.

When we share our humor with others, we share the joy our
heavenly Father has given us.

SHOULDER OF SUPPORT

All of you should be of one mind. Sympathize with each other. Love each other as brothers and sisters. Be tenderhearted, and keep a humble attitude.
1 Peter 3:8 NLT

Our wonderful heavenly Father, the source of all mercy and grace, has demonstrated how to respond to other's adversities. He consoles us in our hardships and sustains us in our trials, teaching us true empathy. When loved ones are in distress, we can offer the same support God has shown us.

If we have experienced similar trials, losses, or difficulties, our hearts share our loved ones' pain on a deeper level. We can suggest a course of action that worked for us, or direct our dear ones to a professional for help. At times, advice won't do. A shoulder to cry on or a sympathetic ear is needed.

The Lord God has loved us with an everlasting love and gently comforted us in our most difficult times so that we can be a shoulder of support for others.

DRESSING UP

I also want the women to dress modestly, with decency and propriety, adorning themselves, not with elaborate hairstyles or gold or pearls or expensive clothes.
1 TIMOTHY 2:9 NIV

Paul addressed the issue of women's clothing to warn the early believers not to dress like the ungodly society in which they lived. Roman women wore their hair in elaborate braids and their flashy jewelry and lavish clothing made a bold statement about their priorities and consideration for others.

This remains a valid concern today. How do we differ from the modern-day unbelievers who live around us? God has no problem with expression and creativity in our clothing selections. His concern is that we choose clothing that is modest and would not cause temptation for those who see us.

The Lord looks at our hearts, and not our clothing. But what we wear reflects what's in our hearts. When we dress modestly, we convey a tender and serene attitude that shows consideration for others. This is precious in the sight of the Lord, and it sets us apart.

IN RUNNING ERRANDS

*As you share your faith with others, I pray that they may come to
know all the blessings Christ has given us.*
PHILEMON 1:6 CEV

We can brighten someone's day with a smile and a kind word. All
of us need to be acknowledged, especially the "invisible" workers
we see each day as we run our errands. It's easy to be annoyed
when one of these individuals doesn't do their job in a satisfactory
manner or seems rude or dismissive. But in every case, we should
look at these encounters as opportunities to share our faith.

Even when service personnel, cashiers, and clerks are being
helpful and polite, it's easy to ignore them when we're rushed. But
when we smile, call them by name, and say, "Thank you," we are
often afforded the privilege of introducing our good God—maybe
just a word or two—to someone.

As Christians, our actions do matter. Our kindness and patience
demonstrate Christ in us. Let's always make sure that we bless
others, even those who are "invisible."

HOSTING A BIBLE STUDY

If anyone comes to your meeting and does not teach the truth
about Christ, don't invite that person into your home
or give any kind of encouragement.
2 John 1:10 NLT

During the first century after Christ's resurrection and ascension, Christians had no church buildings. They met in homes of other believers to learn about and worship the Lord Jesus Christ.

Even though we worship in churches today, many of us come together in our homes for additional discussions. A small group might meet in a restaurant. If weather permits, some study at a picnic table in a public park. We want to learn all we can about God's miraculous Word.

The apostle John's warning about false teachers is as valid now as it was in his day. He feared, as we do now, that those who don't acknowledge Christ's indwelling of the flesh will slip in as wolves to steal the truth. As we study the Scriptures together, we may bring someone who has gone astray back to the truth. Or we may be able to expose a false teacher as we rightly divide the Word of Truth.

CLASS REUNION

*King Nebuchadnezzar of Babylonia had captured many of the
people of Judah and had taken them as prisoners to Babylonia.
Now they were on their way back to Jerusalem and to their own
towns everywhere in Judah.*

EZRA 2:1 CEV

My first question at my last high school reunion was, "Who are
these old people?" Some classmates had actually aged well. Others
gained or lost weight. A few still held a resemblance to their senior
photo, which our hosts mercifully attached to our nametags.

While attending the reunion, I struggled with feelings of both
joy and dread. We left our classmates for a higher education or
careers. Now we returned with our success stories or tales of miss-
spent adulthood.

After seventy years of Babylonian captivity, the Israelites
returned with a combination of joy and dread. Freed by King
Cyrus, they came home to desolation and ruin. But they rebuilt
the temple and re-established the consecrated festivals to honor
the Most High God.

They set a wonderful example to follow. We don't have a
temple to rebuild, but we can re-establish Christian connections and
share our faith with our former classmates.

A GOOD NAME

"Don't be afraid, my daughter. I will do for you whatever you say, since all the people in my town know that you are a woman of noble character."
RUTH 3:11 HCSB

Ruth made an impression on the people in Bethlehem. As a widow, she could have remained with her family in Moab. Instead she moved to a strange land with her widowed mother-in-law, Naomi. She gained a worthy reputation by her hard work in the fields. Her intention was to glean enough food for Naomi and herself. But God allowed her to glean a husband in the process.

Her descendant, King Solomon, stated in his Proverbs that a good name is to be more desired than great riches. Her example of noble character continued through the bloodline of Obed, the child she bore to her husband Boaz.

How do we want to be known by others? Responsible, truthful, unwavering in our faith are all sought-after qualities. We want to follow Ruth's example, gaining the respect of those around us and building a reputation that will bring honor to our family's name.

Discovering God In Family Relationships

MARRIAGE—A NEW IDENTITY

For this reason a man shall leave his father and his mother, and be joined to his wife; and they shall become one flesh.
GENESIS 2:24 NASB

The wedding vows are sealed with a prayer. The honeymoon is over. It's time to adjust to the expectations of a new spouse. We experience changes so subtly; they aren't noticeable right away. With new responsibilities comes a new level of maturity. We think differently about certain issues, coordinate plans to fit our spouse's needs, and consult our spouse before making important decisions. We've assumed a new identity.

We become a new person, too, when we accept the precious gift of salvation from Jesus Christ. Our attitudes change toward life issues. We rearrange our schedules to spend time with the Lord through His Word and worship services. Decisions once made on our own are now prayerfully brought before the Lord for His counsel. We learn to depend on Him for our provisions.

On our wedding day, we changed our status from single to married. When we accepted our Savior, our position changed from lost to found. Our union with Christ is truly a marriage made in heaven.

FOR BETTER OR WORSE

Love cannot be drowned by oceans or floods;
it cannot be bought, no matter what is offered.
SONG OF SOLOMON 8:7 CEV

My husband's personality changed in the span of a few months. We began to have the same conversations over and over again. His mood switched from happy to angry faster than the pendulum on my grandfather clock. Hallucinations swept over him without warning. Gaps in his memory became more frequent.

As his memory loss grew more acute, a tidal wave of panic washed over me. Did he have the dreaded "A" disease? Would he forget me, too?

A referral to a neurologist dammed up the surge of fear, for a while. In the tempest of brain scans, sleep studies, and EEGs, the Lord sheltered me in His peace. Oceans of medical appointments, floods of tests, or the accompanying stress could not drown my love for my husband.

When we are thrust into the role of caregiver for an ailing spouse, the Comforter will throw us a lifeline. Resting on the Father's strength, we can withstand the effects of our beloved's illness, for better or worse.

BIRTHS AND MIRACLES

When Elizabeth heard Mary's greeting, the baby leaped in her womb; and Elizabeth was filled with the Holy Spirit.

LUKE 1:41 NASB

Pregnancy is a series of miracles. First the male and female cells unite to become one. Then the zygotes implant. Even the mother's age can point to a miracle. The biblical account of the advent of Christ notes the contrast of a young girl and an old woman, both pregnant through the grace of God.

Mary, being pure in heart and body, served as the perfect vessel to bring our Savior into the world. Her unquestioning faith in God allowed the miracle of conception to occur without a husband's involvement.

Elizabeth's advanced age added yet another burden to her infertility. But God broke through all the barriers of her empty womb to further His plan. John, the voice of one crying in the wilderness, had to be born. He chose Zacharias and Elizabeth because of their righteousness and adherence to the commandments. They would teach John well.

God set in place the phenomenal conditions for a child to be born, and then by His hand even more miracles followed.

PRECIOUS GIFTS

*Behold, children are a gift of the L*ORD*,*
the fruit of the womb is a reward.
P*SALM* 127:3 NASB

Watching children play and hearing their laughter and squeals of delight make us smile. Little ones turn every day into an adventure, reminding us how life appeared before we grew up and lost our sense of wonder.

Jesus welcomed the little children to come to Him. He lifted them up as examples because of their unsullied trust and belief.

King Solomon viewed them as arrows in the hand of a warrior, not as offensive weapons, but to defend and protect their parents in old age.

God preserved His heritage by commanding Adam to be fruitful and multiply. While children carry many ancestral traits to future generations, each child has his or her own God-given character. Even identical twins have slight differences. Like snowflakes in winter, every child is a unique creation.

Children are beloved in the eyes of the Lord, and training up these precious gifts in the love of our heavenly Father gives honor to Him, our Wonderful Benefactor.

FATHERS, DADDIES, AND PAPAS

As for me and my house, we will serve the Lord.
JOSHUA 24:15 KJV

As leader of his household, a father is duty-bound by Scripture to bring up his children in the reverence of God. He is a visual rendering of the Almighty over His creation.

Three of our friends have differing parental roles. One, separated from his son through divorce, sacrificed his own worldly pursuits to be near the boy. He is a father.

Another married a woman with two children. He adopted them. He and his wife had three more children, giving him both adoptive and biological status. He is a daddy.

The third friend also married a woman with children. He loves them as his own, even though parental rights issues prevent him from adopting them. He is a papa.

These three men have one thing in common: the decision to serve the Lord in their households. They provide a godly role model for the children. They understand the urgency of teaching the next generation to praise the Lord for His strength and wondrous works.

God's love shines through fathers, daddies, and papas when they choose to serve Him.

FAMILY HARMONY

Children, obey your parents in the Lord: for this is right.
EPHESIANS 6:1 KJV

A man gave his three-year old daughter a little spank on her diapered bottom for misbehaving. She surprised him by spanking him back on his bare arm. He sent her to her room, stating firmly, "Little girls don't spank their daddies."

When he allowed her to come back out, she looked up at him with her big doe eyes and asked, "Who spanks daddies when they're bad?"

After mulling her question over in his mind, he finally answered, "God spanks daddies and mommies when they do wrong."

Thankfully, the little girl didn't pursue the subject any further, and the family harmony was restored—at least for a while.

We all come into this world wired with rebellious traits that did not come from our perfect Creator. We inherited our defiance from Adam and Eve, who learned it from the enemy of our souls, Satan.

We don't like punishing our children, and God takes no pleasure in disciplining us. But sometimes it's necessary to preserve harmony in the family of God.

FAMILY SEPARATIONS

Perhaps he was for this reason separated from you for a while,
that you would have him back forever.
PHILEMON 1:15 NASB

When children leave home for college or career opportunities, the households they leave behind echo with their absence. Letting go requires a giant step for parents.

Other separations occur within families. Siblings marry or move across the country. Empty nesters relocate to a milder climate. Military service separates husbands and wives during long deployments. We, like the apostle Paul, should look for a deeper purpose in God's sovereignty when circumstances take us from our loved ones.

Paul explained to Philemon the true reason Onesimus ran away. On the surface, it appeared as an act of disobedience. But God brought the slave to Paul to learn about Christ. He returned to serve with an obedient heart knowing Philemon would treat him as a brother.

When we kiss our dear ones goodbye, we can be assured our Lord has a purpose for that venture. It may be for our spiritual growth or theirs—or both. He alone knows the reason. We can put our loved ones in His capable hands.

FAMILY REUNIONS

If Saul wonders where I am, tell him, "David asked me to let him go to his hometown of Bethlehem, so he could take part in a sacrifice his family makes there every year."
1 Samuel 20:6 CEV

Not so long ago, it was common for generations of families to remain in the same area. But after World War II, that changed. Many soldiers came home only long enough to gather their personal belongings and move away for jobs, to reunite with their brides—or both.

Most families now come together only when it's time to marry or bury a loved one. Even when we're geographically close, the busyness of life often keeps us apart. We often forget the wealth of joy woven into our relationships.

David used the annual sacrifice with his family as an excuse to elude the king's wrath. Today, some of us would rather face angry King Saul than attend a family reunion. We give more weight to the dread of re-opening old wounds than the possibility of finding forgiveness. But the love of our Lord, reflected in His creation of family, ties us to each other. We can reunite, reconnect, and re-establish the bond of family when we come together, from near or far, in kindness and love.

FAMILY TRADITIONS

Brethren, stand fast, and hold the traditions which ye have been taught, whether by word, or our epistle.
2 Thessalonians 2:15 KJV

The word *tradition* brings to mind the musical production, *Fiddler on the Roof*. In that story, Tevye, the father, tried in vain to hold fast to the traditions he embraced. He wanted to honor God by passing the precepts and customs to the next generation. But progressive attitudes broke through his protective wall of faith, to the detriment of his impressionable young daughters. His family's way of life crumbled under the stress of changes and anti-Semitic pogroms.

Like Tevye, we are sometimes labeled old fashioned or backward when we adhere to the traditions of our faith. But the Lord expects us to hold fast to them so that He will be glorified in us. He has called us to be His light to the darkened world.

When we uphold our Christian family traditions, such as praying before a meal, we point to our heavenly Father and proclaim we belong to Him. He strengthens our hearts in every good work and word.

WHEN TEMPERS FLARE

Do not be eager in your heart to be angry,
For anger resides in the bosom of fools.
ECCLESIASTES 7:9 NASB

Offering a gentle response to turn away wrath is easier said than done. We can't always be on cloud nine. As life weaves its threads of events through our days, we're bound to hit a snag.

Someone makes a casual remark that knocks us off-center. Our initial reaction might be to lash out with harsh words or merely a stern look. If we take time to consider their words before responding, we could defuse our anger before we hit the ceiling.

Putting the shoe on the other foot, a person might react in anger to our innocent words or actions. Our bright, "Good morning!" might be met with a frown and a grumble. We don't know what millstones may be weighing on someone's heart that might cause him or her to be abrupt or hurtful toward us. Showing mercy is the first step to averting an anger-filled moment.

When we replace anger with love, the flame of resentment dies out. Our Lord has shown us how to do this, for His mercy is everlasting.

A FIRM FOUNDATION

"They are like a man building a house, who dug down deep and laid the foundation on rock. When a flood came, the torrent struck that house but could not shake it, because it was well built."

LUKE 6:48 NIV

Our house, constructed in the 1920s, stands on brick piers. The builders dug deep into the shifting sand to anchor the piers to the rock hidden below. This humble wood-frame bungalow has held up through hurricanes and heavy rains for more than eighty years.

Our families need the same foundational support. Everyone who comes to Jesus and hears His words and acts on them is like the wise builder. We dig through the shifting sands of false teachings to reach the true Word of God. Our households are anchored to the Everlasting Rock. When storms of trouble come like tsunamis with destructive, high winds, our families can cling to the unshakable foundation.

When we hold to our faith in our Savior, the torrents and floods will not shake our families.

A house is sheltered with a roof above;
A home is sheltered with Jesus' love.

SIBLING ALLIANCE

*"Whoever does the will of God, he is My brother
and sister and mother."*
MARK 3:35 NASB

My brother and sister and I fought like enemies during our childhood, until someone threatened us. My sister defended me against a name-calling classmate. My brother confronted a bully who picked on me. Being the baby of the family, I secretly idolized my siblings.

As teenagers, my sister and I squabbled over bedroom territory, but shared our clothing. Our brother, a black belt in karate, changed his role from tormentor to protector.

Now that we're adults, we share a bond that neither distance nor duty can break. We don't see each other often; but in difficult times, we've got each other's backs.

When we do the will of God, we become brothers and sisters in Christ. Belonging to His family turns our sibling rivalry into sibling alliance. We comfort each other in need and encourage each other in success.

Blood may be thicker than water, but Christ is more binding than blood. We are Christian allies, not worldly rivals.

RESPECTING OUR ELDERS

*Older men are to be level headed, worthy of respect, sensible, and
sound in faith, love, and endurance. In the same way, older women
are to be reverent in behavior, not slanderers, not addicted to much
wine. They are to teach what is good.*

TITUS 2:2–3 HCSB

Many seniors carry a full load of responsibilities. Although some
have retired from their paid positions, they still work at setting a
good example for younger family members. They bear the scars
of the spiritual and emotional battles we now face and offer their
experiential advice. Some have homegrown remedies for what ails
us. Others are "hands-on" experts on making something new or
repairing something old.

We look to them for wisdom in matters of the heart and soul.
They've had more time to study the Bible and spent more hours
on their knees in prayer. In practice, they show younger men and
women how we are to treat each other.

When we don't have answers for our thought-provoking
questions, it's often our elders who direct us to the book of divine
solutions—the Word of God. In that act alone, they prove their
wisdom and are worthy of our respect.

BLESSINGS OF MOTHERS-IN-LAW

Ruth said, "...Where you go, I will go, and where you lodge, I will lodge. Your people shall be my people, and your God, my God."
RUTH 1:16 NASB

Recently a newscaster reported the rare catch of a goblin shark in the Gulf of Mexico. He laughed and quoted the fisherman's comment, "It's uglier than my mother-in-law." There is also a plant with barbed red flowers growing at the top called a mother-in-law's tongue.

Mothers-in-law take the brunt of many jokes, but there were at least two who honored God. Naomi showed God's love to both of her daughters-in-law. When her husband and two sons died, and she was preparing to return to Israel, Ruth and Orpah begged to go with her. Jesus healed Peter's mother-in-law of a high fever, and she got up immediately and waited on Him. These mothers-in-law exemplify love and service.

In most cases, mothers-in-law have their child's best interest in mind. What we consider as meddling, they consider as a simple offer to help. Before we criticize them, we should remember that without her, our spouse would not have been born. The Lord gave her a precious gift, which she now shares with us.

AGING GRACEFULLY

*"Even to your old age I will be the same, and even to your
graying years I will bear you!"*
ISAIAH 46:4 NASB

God created Adam and Eve as mature adults. But did He intend for
them to grow old, or is old age another dismal consequence of sin?
The patriarchs' ages and the phrase, ". . .and then he died. . ." are not
listed until after Adam and Eve had fallen for the serpent's lie.

Now aging is inevitable. Proper diet and exercise might delay
the telltale signs. Cosmetic surgery may hide them for a while. And
yet, ignoring the aging process proves more difficult with each
landmark birthday.

On the bright side, each new wrinkle and bout of joint stiffness
should remind us that we have been blessed with long life. When
our hair turns gray and wrinkles etch our faces, our Creator will still
love us and consider us precious. When our eyesight is blurry and
our hearing is weak, when we shuffle our steps and forget events,
our Lord will bear us up. And He has promised that one day we will
receive new bodies that will not age at all.

GOING HOME AGAIN

*Just let me return to my hometown, where I can someday
be buried near my father and mother.*
2 Samuel 19:37 cev

My husband, Tom, and I visited his hometown. As we drove through
the old neighborhood with his sister and brother-in-law, Tom
stopped in front of a two-story house. He and his sister both stared
at the home with nostalgic awe. We all climbed out of our car when
a man came out through the front door.

Tom approached him. "I was born in that house."

The man smiled and offered to let us walk through it. "But
first," he said, "would you be Tommy?" He pointed to a tiny
handprint in the concrete driveway with the name printed above it.

Of course, my husband can't go back to being little Tommy
who immortalized his existence with a handprint. But he can revisit
the sweet memories and thank God for a childhood lived out in a
loving family.

The circumstances of our lives here on earth vary greatly. But
each of us carries a memory of some cherished blessing for which
we can thank God.

Discovering God In Sickness And In Health

HOSPITALS

A man from Samaria then came traveling along that road. When he saw the man, he felt sorry for him and went over to him. He treated his wounds with olive oil and wine and bandaged them. Then he put him on his own donkey and took him to an inn, where he took care of him.

LUKE 10:33–34 CEV

The inn where the man from Samaria took the injured victim might be considered the first hospital. The Samaritan served as the first EMT, with his donkey as the ambulance. Then he became doctor and nurse in follow-up care.

Our medical facilities are more sophisticated now with radiology, surgery, and trauma care; to name only a few of the many departments.

Whether we work in a hospital, visit loved ones there, or are admitted for our own ailments, we can feel the Lord's presence if we look for Him. He stands with the nurse taking the patient's vitals. He guides the surgeon's hands in the operating room. He comforts the person in pain. He takes the hand of the one passing into eternity. He heals all patients, either by restoring them to physical health or perfecting them for heaven.

PERSISTENT THORNS

He has said to me, "My grace is sufficient for you,
for power is perfected in weakness."
2 CORINTHIANS 12:9 NASB

Chronic pain and ailments can strain our faith in the Lord. We pray for relief, but when it doesn't come, we wonder if our faith is strong enough. After all, Christ restored sight to the blind and cleansed the lepers. The lame walked, and the deaf heard. He even raised Lazarus from the dead. Yet we continue to suffer.

The woman with a continuous hemorrhage experienced healing at the mere touch of Jesus' robe. But she had endured the bleeding for twelve years before meeting Him.

Paul asked three times to be relieved of his affliction, and the Lord denied his pleas. The apostle considered the thorn in his flesh the work of Satan, which God allowed to keep him humble. Paul accepted the distress the thorn caused him with joy. It forced him to lean more fully on the Lord.

When we are at our weakest and must utterly rely on our Lord, He gives us His strength to endure. God's grace is sufficient for us, especially in chronic ailments.

RECUPERATING

Beloved, I pray that in all respects you may prosper and be in good health, just as your soul prospers.

3 JOHN 2 NASB

Most of us have experienced the serious injury or critical illness of a loved one. In those early days, we pray fervently for that first decisive improvement. We rejoice and give thanks as we should, but we sometimes forget that a long road of recovery still lies ahead.

Rehabilitation can take many forms—rebuilding strength in legs and arms, learning to speak again, and learning new skills to replace those lost. The need for prayers continues during this painful and often frustrating time. The physical effort, along with the associated pain, and setbacks in progress are discouraging.

It's important for prayers to continue during this time—prayers for endurance, for progress, and for encouragement. Even if the process doesn't completely restore our loved one, we still give thanks for every little step forward. Our Lord has given us the ability to flourish in difficulty and thrive in suffering when we put our trust in Him. Being constant in prayer for our loved ones gives us the opportunity to grow in maturity in love and faith.

BROKEN BONES

Again He said to me, "Prophesy over these bones and say to them,
'O dry bones, hear the word of the LORD.' "

EZEKIEL 37:4 NASB

A friend tripped going down a flight of stairs, resulting in a break
in the shin. Another friend broke her forearm playing golf. Both
incidents required x-rays to determine the appropriate treatment,
followed by a cast and orders not to use the injured limb for a
specified period of time.

These injuries remind us of our flawed condition. God created
us in a perfect state. But when sin entered, we became fragile and
easily broken. In response, God set a natural healing process into
motion. When our damaged bones are correctly set and protected,
they miraculously knit themselves back together.

Similarly, in Ezekiel's vision, the dry bones in the valley
became whole. While this prophetic revelation illustrated the
future restoration of Israel, it also depicts how the Lord restores
our fractured lives. By His command, the skeletons in the valley
reconnected. And by His command, our deep cracks are restored.

As we revere the Lord and listen for His Word, we will be
healed, in body and spirit.

EYEGLASSES

I pray that the eyes of your heart may be enlightened, so that you will know what is the hope of His calling.
EPHESIANS 1:18 NASB

Eyeglasses were designed to help us overcome our visual handicaps, bringing into view what failing eyesight conceals. As early as 700 BC, the Assyrians used polished crystal to magnify objects. A thousand years later, the invention of clear, well-ground glass became the newest reading aid. Benjamin Franklin invented the bifocal in 1784.

Even with corrective lenses, stress and fatigue can cause us to see things that aren't really there and overlook things that are. The phrase "seeing is believing" isn't always true.

Believing doesn't have to come through sight. Jesus said to Thomas, "Blessed are they who did not see, and yet believed." When we open the eyes of our hearts, we see by faith. None of us has come face-to-face with the Lord Jesus Christ, but now that we're new creations in Him, we rejoice in the glory of His love.

God's Light shines through us, and our hearts clearly see the hope of His calling.

LIVING LONG IN PROSPERITY

"If you walk in My ways, keeping My statutes and commandments,
as your father David walked, then I will prolong your days."
1 KINGS 3:14 NASB

A local newspaper reporter interviewed our neighbor on her
hundredth birthday. When he asked to what she attributed her long
life, she told the young whippersnapper that she read her Bible and
prayed every day. In her tireless efforts to tell others about the love
of Christ, she was a remarkable example of a faithful servant to
the Lord. The century in which she lived bore its share of tragedies,
but the blessings she witnessed far outweighed them. The most
important to her was the use of new technologies to spread the
message of God's love through Jesus Christ.

This sweet, godly woman lived to be one hundred and four
years old, passing quietly into the arms of the Lord while holding
her beloved pet. God had rewarded her faithfulness with a long and
happy life.

We never retire from walking in the ways of God. Even beyond
this mortal life, we will rejoice in doing the will of our Father in
heaven.

Discovering God In Tragedies

WHEN DISASTER STRIKES

*After you have suffered for a little while, the God of all grace,
who called you to His eternal glory in Christ, will Himself perfect,
confirm, strengthen and establish you.*
1 PETER 5:10 NASB

An explosion rocks a western town. Tornadoes rip through an
elementary school. A boat sinks with hundreds of passengers
onboard. Disaster strikes with the speed and venom of a rattlesnake,
turning our lives upside down. We want the world to stop spinning,
at least long enough for us to grasp the reality of what has
happened. But life carries on, and so must we.

We can't turn back the clock or pretend the ordeal never
happened. The catastrophe changes us. We live by a different
standard now. But God has not forsaken us. He is here with us as we
pick up the pieces, care for the survivors, and bury the dead.

A new strength emerges within us, a gift from the Holy Spirit.
With an unseen hand propping us up, we move forward. We pray
for courage and wisdom, and probe for answers. Then the Lord
embraces us with His loving arms, and we seek closure for our loss
through Him.

WORRY AND FRET

*We are destroying speculations and every lofty thing raised up
against the knowledge of God, and we are taking every thought
captive to the obedience of Christ.*

2 Corinthians 10:5 NASB

Those bandits—Worry and his cousin Fret—break in through an
unlocked window of our minds to steal our joy.

"Give me your energy," Worry demands. "Give me your time."

Fret jabs us with speculations, "What if—?" and lists the worst
things that can happen.

They want to confine us to their prison of hollow and
deceptive anxiety. "We want all your attention," they chant in
unison. "Worship us."

We loosen their stranglehold when we cry out to the Lord.
Our loving Father rescues us with His words of truth. Hope-filled
Scriptures, our weapons against the bandits, are powerful enough
to breach their fortress.

Our faith gives us strength and courage to say to these joy-
robbers, "You are not my god. I will not worship you." In this way,
we are able to escape the snares of the devil. Discouraging thoughts
thrown at us in distressing circumstances no longer control us. We
take them captive to the obedience of Christ.

HEROES

The priest of Midian had seven daughters: and they came and drew water, and filled the troughs to water their father's flock. And the shepherds came and drove them away: but Moses stood up and helped them, and watered their flock.
Exodus 2:16–17 KJV

Firefighters, police officers, and soldiers put their lives on the line daily to rescue, protect, and defend us. They heed the call of duty with little regard for their own safety. These heroes act as our "shield wall" of protection.

There are other heroes who also save people from harm. These individuals may have no professional training at all. They simply see a need, like Moses did, and step in to help without being asked and often without expecting a reward.

The greatest hero of all, Jesus Christ, stepped into our world, humbled Himself in obedience to the point of death, even death on a cross. He rescued us from eternal separation from our Creator, Almighty God. When our enemy, Satan, tries to drive us away from our living water, Jesus intervenes on our behalf and waters His flock. He who is highly exalted, gave His life to rescue, protect, and defend us.

STOLEN TREASURES

"Do not store up for yourselves treasures on earth, where moth and rust destroy, and where thieves break in and steal."
MATTHEW 6:19 NASB

When my indoor cats met me in the driveway, and I found the front door half-way open, I immediately phoned the sheriff's office.

The deputy arrived, made sure the burglars had gone, and began dusting for fingerprints. But the windowsill yielded only paw prints. The burglars had left no identifying clues behind. An assessment of what was missing included heirloom jewelry. A number of antique pieces set with precious gemstones passed down through generations into my care—gone. My late parents' rings that had brought joyful memories—gone. My life's treasures, now in the possession of uncaring reprobates, lost to me forever.

Though I was shaken by the crime, the Lord opened my eyes. My deceased family members in heaven would not be angry with me for letting their jewels fall into evil hands. They wouldn't want me to cling to material things. Jewelry is fleeting and elusive, but no burglar can steal my heavenly treasures. No one can take away the joy of my faith. My reverence of God, my heavenly treasure—here, forever.

HEARTBREAK

He heals the brokenhearted and binds up their wounds.
PSALM 147:3 NASB

We feel most vulnerable when our hearts are broken. But God has not deserted us. Christ endured every heartbreaking situation we will ever experience.

- Loneliness—Jesus spent forty days alone in the wilderness, being tempted by the devil.
- Loss of home and possessions—Jesus had nowhere to lay His head.
- Death of a friend or loved one—Jesus wept quietly in grief before bringing Lazarus back to life.
- When everyone turns against us—Jesus wept bitterly over the city of Jerusalem, knowing they would shun Him.
- Betrayal—Judas Iscariot took a bribe to hand Jesus over to the enemy.
- Anguish—Jesus fell on His face and prayed for the cup of suffering to pass from Him.
- The death of a child; nothing is more devastating—God gave His Son to die for us.
- In extreme pain—Jesus endured the agony of the crucifixion.
- Abandonment—Jesus was alone on the cross. God had to turn away when Christ took on Himself the sins of the world.

God took on human form, suffered for us, and now binds up our wounds and heals our broken hearts with His deep, eternal love.

DEATH

Just as through one man sin entered into the world, and death through sin, and so death spread to all men, because all sinned.
ROMANS 5:12 NASB

Death is inevitable, but not what God wanted for His creation. His desire for us has always been eternal life. He loves us and wants us to spend forever with Him.

When Adam and Eve rebelled against God's authority, they corrupted the perfect world He created for them. Death entered Eden, separating mankind from the loving Father. This deep chasm created by sin has been passed down through generations, giving death an iron grip on us.

The devil thought he had won when Christ died on the cross. But His resurrection obliterated the stronghold of sin and death. Through Him our first and last enemy has been abolished.

Our deaths now are merely separations from the physical relationships we share with our loved ones. We know we will be with Christ in heaven because of our trust and faith in Him. O death, where is your victory? O death, where is your sting?

IN MOURNING

"Blessed are those who mourn, for they shall be comforted."
MATTHEW 5:4 NASB

I was five years old when my granddaddy suddenly passed away.
For a few weeks after the funeral, my sister and I took turns staying
overnight with my grandmother. Our presence during that difficult
time was a balm to her healing. Her anticipation of a future reunion
in heaven with her husband helped ease the pain, too.

No one escapes mourning. We all have lost or will lose
someone dear to us. Grieving alone deepens the sorrow. God has
put friends and family members in our lives who want to comfort
us. It's His blessing.

As we console our grief-stricken loved one, words may not be
necessary. Sometimes a hug is the only communication they need.
We show the love of Christ in times of grief when we sit with them
and let them talk, or let them cry, or cry with them.

We know that God will wipe away every tear from our eyes,
and there will no longer be any death; there will no longer be any
mourning or crying or pain. He is our Comfort.

BE NOT DISMAYED

*He said. . . "'Do not fear or be dismayed because of this great
multitude, for the battle is not yours but God's.'"*
2 CHRONICLES 20:15 NASB

Our struggles can overwhelm us. The fear of "what-ifs" can swallow
up our hope and leave us feeling alone and vulnerable.

Jehoshaphat, king of Judah, was greatly dismayed when he
learned of the armies coming to make war against him. His kingdom
was powerless in the face of such great numbers. In his distress, he
turned to the Lord and prayed. His prayer summed up all that the
Most High God had done for His people. Jehoshaphat admitted that
he was powerless and didn't know what to do.

His statement, "Our eyes are on You," serves as a strong
reminder for us to look to the Lord for help when overwhelming
circumstances come against us. We can give our distress to God,
for the battle is not ours, but His. The Lord might tell us—as He did
Jehoshaphat—to go out to face the enemy, for He is with us. All
power and might are in His hands. Then and now, no one can stand
against Him.

Discovering God In Communication

PHONE HOME

"Job said, 'The ear tests the words it hears just as the mouth distinguishes between foods.' So let us discern for ourselves what is right; let us learn together what is good."

JOB 34:3-4 NLT

In the BCP era (before cell phones), our friends provided their teenaged daughter with a phone card as she boarded a bus for a week-long music competition. They waited for word of her safe arrival, but none came. Checking with other parents, they learned the group had reached their destination. Their daughter didn't call once during the week.

Upon her return, our friends confronted their daughter, and she admitted she had chosen not to call. Rehearsals, performances, and time with friends demanded her attention. She had been too busy.

There are times when thinking, *I'm too busy,* means I've chosen not to call on my heavenly Father. Even though I know He longs to hear from me, life's distractions offer a thousand reasons to ignore this great privilege. It's something we all struggle with. But when we do put other things aside and take time with Him, we are the ones who are blessed.

MAIL DELIVERY

We do not know what to pray for as we should, but the Spirit
Himself intercedes for us with unspoken groanings.
ROMANS 8:26 HCSB

We send mail expecting it to reach its destination on time. Only
during state-declared emergencies has the postal service strayed
from its "neither snow, nor rain, nor gloom of night" refrain.

Sometimes we need confirmation that the addressee receives
our letter. Tracking devices add to the postage, but the peace of
mind is worth it. Mail is returned to us for insufficient postage or
a wrong address. We correct and resend it, but our error delays the
delivery.

Our prayers are special letters to our heavenly Father. We send
Him praises, petitions, and notes of appreciation. We don't need
special functions to ensure He receives our mail. Our prayers aren't
returned to us if we fail to put a stamp on them. Jesus already paid
the postage for us. And God's address is always the same: heaven.

The Holy Spirit delivers our letters to God regardless
of inclement weather, disastrous events, or our inability to
articulate our thoughts. Even when we muddle our prayers, He
intercedes for us.

IN THE NEWS

They reported to the Angel of the LORD standing among the myrtle
trees, "We have patrolled the earth, and right now
the whole earth is calm and quiet."
ZECHARIAH 1:11 HCSB

"The whole earth is calm and quiet," are words we'll probably never hear from the news media. Strife sells. Without wars and rumors of wars, earthquakes in diverse places, famine, and pestilence, the news vendors have nothing to report. In their defense, they sometimes report good deeds and happy endings before turning to more horrific stories. We can't blame them. The fact that good news isn't profitable speaks more about the world we live in than their slant on reporting.

Zechariah's vision asserted that the Lord would restore Israel and that her cities would once again overflow with prosperity. The nation of Israel is the focal point of many news stories today. God still cares deeply for Jacob's descendants. We can see His hand moving events and circumstances toward the day when they will call on His name, and He will answer them; and He will say, "They are My people," and they will say, "The Lord is my God." That will be a great day in the news!

INSTANT COMMUNICATION

*Esther summoned Hathach from the king's eunuchs, whom the king
had appointed to attend her, and ordered him to go to Mordecai to
learn what this was and why it was.*

ESTHER 4:5 NASB

Valuable time ticked by while Esther and Mordecai sent messages
back and forth, using her servants. The edict to annihilate her
people had been signed and sealed. Only through the sovereignty of
God were they able to show King Ahasuerus Haman's treacherous
plot. He couldn't rescind the edict, but he allowed her people to
defend themselves against the coming attack.

A modern-day Mordecai would've sent a text message to
Esther with photos of himself, distressed and wearing sackcloth
and ashes. But this was God's timing. They both needed a period of
fasting and prayer to demonstrate their dependence on the Lord.

We now have instant communication. Through the Internet,
we can see or talk to someone half a world away. In this age of
urgency, are we too rushed to fast and pray for three days as Esther
did? This may be just the right time to step away from the keyboard
and seek God's face.

FACING OUR TWEETS

Tell everyone of every nation, "Praise the glorious power of the Lord."
1 Chronicles 16:28 cev

When King David brought the Ark of the Covenant back, his good news traveled fast. He relied on speedy messengers on horseback to reach those far away. But even the speediest horseman can't compare to the virtually instant communication technologies we have access to today.

Our social media devices provide immediate contact with others. We can use these Internet exchanges as a tool for sharing the Gospel of Jesus Christ with everyone we know. A photograph of a specific page in our Bibles displays a short chapter. Type in a favorite verse to post and watch it get reposted by one friend and then another. It continues on a thread through millions of people sharing our comment.

The Holy Spirit may use our messages to poke someone and get his or her attention. The Lord knows whom He wants to link through us. He provides the means for us to spread the message of grace and save the world—one tweet, post, or pin at a time.

SENDING CARDS AND LETTERS

I felt the necessity to write to you appealing that you contend earnestly
for the faith which was once for all handed down to the saints.
JUDE 1:3 NASB

Written greeting cards and letters have become a rare treat. We rely
so heavily on e-mail and e-cards that we sometimes forget about
people who don't have Internet access. A card or personal note with
a Bible verse in it makes a shut-in's day.

A prison inmate feels alone until receiving a Thinking of You
card or personal note saying that someone is praying for him or her.
A get well card with a prayer enclosed to an ailing neighbor is good
medicine for the soul. When a friend is going through a difficult
time, a condolence card cheers the heart and refreshes hope.

Thank You notes to customers or clients let them know we
appreciate their business. We pick out personalized birthday and
anniversary greetings for our loved ones celebrating their special
events.

As we send comfort to the sick, hope to the downhearted,
and sympathy to the grieving, we proclaim Christ's love. By sharing
happy birthdays and anniversaries, we proclaim His joy.

WHEN OUR FAITH IS CHALLENGED

*The Lord is faithful, and He will strengthen
and protect you from the evil one.*
2 Thessalonians 3:3 NASB

Paul received a disturbing message that evil men had entered the church in Thessalonica and perverted his message. He encouraged the believers to hold firm to the truth and shun the deceivers. From the beginning of God's church, unbelievers have challenged our faith.

Confrontations come against Christians every day. Atheists file frivolous lawsuits. Skeptics petition legislation to change laws, and cynics resort to name-calling in their efforts to silence us. In other countries, faithful believers' lives are in danger. As our fellow believers today stand on the promises of God, unyielding in their faith, God uses their bravery to bring others to salvation.

God has called us to tell of His wondrous love. His strength emboldens us to face all challengers. The evil one holds no power over us, for God keeps us under His protective arm, and gives us the most powerful defensive weapon we can use—His Word of truth.

Discovering God In Walls

TEARING DOWN WALLS

When the people heard the sound of the trumpet, the people
shouted with a great shout and the wall fell down flat.
JOSHUA 6:20 NASB

"Mr. Gorbachev, tear down this wall!"

On June 12, 1987, President Reagan issued this challenge to Soviet Union leader Gorbachev in a speech at the Brandenburg Gate near the Berlin Wall. The Berlin Wall, erected August 13, 1961, symbolized an imprisoned people in the post-World War II Eastern bloc.

On November 9, 1989, the Wall and the borders opened. I'll never forget the tears of joy in my father's eyes that day. He fought to free the oppressed, only to see them pushed deeper into the mire of anti-God tyranny.

We sometimes feel like we're butting up against the Berlin Wall when we try to reach loved ones for Jesus Christ. They resist, unwilling to listen to a message that we know will bring them joy and newfound freedom. But we can't challenge them the way Reagan confronted Gorbachev. Taking a cue from Joshua, we can learn a different way to tear down their defenses. He consulted the Lord and followed His directions. So can we.

MEMORIAL WALLS

"Do not rejoice in this, that the spirits are subject to you, but rather rejoice because your names are written in heaven."
LUKE 10:20 NKJV

We erect memorial walls engraved with the names of soldiers who served in wars, first responders and victims who suffered violence or disasters, and for those who died for their Christian faith. There are even walls to remember the unborn. These loving gestures honor those we've lost.

Stephen, the first disciple martyred for teaching about Christ, asked the Lord not to hold the sin of his murder against his assailants. He received more than a commemorative wall. The Lord Jesus Christ stood to welcome him into the Kingdom of God.

In 1956, Jim Elliot, Nate Saint, Pete Fleming, Roger Youderian, and Ed McCully were slaughtered while attempting to evangelize natives in Ecuador. They didn't use deadly weapons to defend themselves because the natives weren't ready for death. Their attitude of forgiveness reflects their love for Christ.

It appears these martyrs lost the battle against evil, but their deaths proclaim victory. Their names are inscribed on the most magnificent memorial wall—in heaven.

Discovering God In Signs

SIGNS TO GUIDE US

"In the morning, 'there will be a storm today, for the sky is red and threatening.' Do you know how to discern the appearance of the sky, but cannot discern the signs of the times?"
MATTHEW 16:3 NASB

Signs on the highways guide us as we travel, indicating the miles to the correct exit for our destination. Without them we might wonder if we've driven too far out of the way or inadvertently made a wrong turn. We begin to fret and then we see it—that long-awaited sign. Our confidence returns; yes, we're on the right road.

When the scribes and Pharisees demanded Jesus prove He was the Messiah, He pointed to Jonah. A direction from the past pointed to the world's future. Both spent three days in a dark place to bring us out of judgment and condemnation.

Jesus has already given us His long-awaited signs of the times. The cross represents His sacrifice. The rolled-away stone proclaims His victory over death. And the Bible reassures us when we doubt. Our confidence returns; yes, we're on the road to heaven.

BILLBOARDS

*The Lord said to me, "Write my answer plainly on tablets, so that a
runner can carry the correct message to others."*
HABAKKUK 2:2 NLT

An anonymous benefactor paid to have biblical references printed
on billboards throughout the countryside. Some bore scripture
verses, while others displayed short quips. "Don't make me
come down there. . .again" was my favorite. These signs provided
humorous relief from the ads for motels, car dealerships, and other
merchants along our highways. They also reminded us that we have
a loving heavenly Father.

The Lord instructed Habakkuk to write his vision in large
and clear lettering for easy comprehension. Because God loved
His people, He warned them of the coming punishment for their
infidelity. Vengeance would come in a fury against the Israelites
who practiced idolatry.

Habakkuk's prophecy that the "earth will be filled with the
knowledge of the glory of the Lord, as the waters cover the sea" will
occur in God's appointed time. He uses every means available, even
modern billboards, to point us back to the Bible so we can rush to
tell others.

PROHIBITION SIGNS

You have died with Christ, and he has set you free from the spiritual
powers of this world. So why do you keep on following the rules of
the world, such as, "Don't handle! Don't taste! Don't touch!"?
COLOSSIANS 2:20–21 NLT

DO NOT ENTER, NO TRESPASSING, HIGH VOLTAGE are examples of some
prohibition signs we run across in our daily activities. They're posted
for our safety or to protect another's property. Consequences, as
mild as a warning or as severe as personal injury, arise when we
don't comply with these notices.

False teachers in Colossae had prohibition signs that benefited
their own schemes. They promoted heretical teachings, which
constrained the new believers' worship. The apostle Paul reminded
them that Christ's sacrifice freed them from ritualistic practices.

This epistle alerts us to the enemy who sneaks these myths
into our churches today. Severe legalistic restrictions hinder our
worship of the King of kings and cause us to focus on the law
instead of our Lord. He who slithers in unnoticed like a serpent tries
in vain to nullify Jesus' work on the cross.

Obeying prohibition signs in our communities protects us. But
in our worship, Christ is sufficient.

Discovering God In Property

REBUILDING A CHURCH

Thus says the Lord of hosts, "Consider your ways! Go up to the mountains, bring wood and rebuild the temple, that I may be pleased with it and be glorified," says the Lord.
HAGGAI 1:7–8 NASB

A time-weary church stands neglected due to a lack of money or manpower. Empty pews need to be filled with people hungry for God's Word. The church body needs help.

The Israelites returning from Babylon were excited about rebuilding the temple. But life's distractions tempered their zeal, delaying the renovation another fifteen years. They tended to their own day-to-day obligations instead of taking care of the Lord's interests.

Our heavenly Father gives us opportunities to check our priorities. He puts us in situations where we have to choose between serving Him and tending to our own needs. Putting ourselves first brings dissatisfaction. Hard work produces little progress. When we serve Him, even when we gain little material wealth, He blesses us with joy.

As we consider our ways, we give careful thought about our priorities and look for means to align them with God's. Then He will help us rebuild our church body.

DEMOLISHING THE OLD; MAKING WAY FOR THE NEW

A time to tear down and a time to build up.

ECCLESIASTES 3:3 NASB

Living in an older part of a city, we see small, quaint homes marked for demolition every day. The out-of-date houses have long since passed their usefulness. They creak and groan as their archaic foundations bear the weight of hardened wood frames. Each one is reduced to rubble and then hauled away in pieces. Soon, a new multi-story mansion with modern conveniences will replace the tiny two-bedroom bungalow. Little by little, the neighborhood is transformed.

As I watch the wrecking crew, I consider my own earthy house, the physical body I rent from my Creator. As it ages, it creaks and groans under the stress of everyday activities I could easily manage in my younger days. My spirit is willing, but the structure is weak.

One day, I'll shed this old, perishable structure. In the twinkling of an eye, I will put on my new immortal mansion. No more groans or creaks, just rejoicing in the glory of the Lord.

RENOVATIONS

*Then he showed me another vision. I saw the Lord standing beside
a wall that had been built using a plumb line. He was using a
plumb line to see if it was still straight.*

AMOS 7:7 NLT

My handy-man husband uses a plumb line in our home renovations.
Our old bungalow came with multiple restoration needs. He
checked the straightness of the walls before we bought the house.
Misalignments make repairs difficult, if not impossible. But they
were straight and true, giving us the green light to make the
purchase.

God appraised the nation of Israel with a plumb line. He
measured them against His law. In their prosperity and great
power, under Jeroboam's rule, they shunned the Lord and clung
to idolatry. Amos made a desperate plea for them to repent as the
only means to hold back the coming judgment. But they stood
firmly against him.

Our plumb line today is the cross. Jesus said to love God with
all our heart, soul, mind, and strength. We can keep the plumb line
of our lives straight and true with our love for Christ, our salvation
through Him, our study of His Word, and our steadfast faith in God.

USING POWER TOOLS

He did not know that the LORD had departed from him.
JUDGES 16:20 NASB

Rather than unplug and re-plug the vacuum cleaner when I move from room to room on cleaning day, I leave it plugged in to the same outlet. The cord is then stretched as far as it will reach. The vacuum cleaner quits in the middle of the job, and I find the cord on the floor, ripped from the outlet. My cleaning tool is useless without electricity.

Samson, in his arrogance, stretched the power of the Holy Spirit too far and became unplugged. He couldn't rely on his own human strength to defend himself against his attackers, and they captured him. While in their prison, he cried out to God. The Lord gave him enough strength to destroy the Philistines' house, guests, and pagan idol.

We can be God's tools only when we remain plugged in to His higher power. When we stretch ourselves out too far and sever our connection with His protective hand, we can cry out to Him to be restored. He gives strength to the weary and to him who lacks might, He increases power.

BUYING AND SELLING

*Jesus said to them, "Render to Caesar the things that are Caesar's,
and to God the things that are God's."*
MARK 12:17 NASB

A friend's vehicle he had driven for the past ten years finally quit
and was deemed unrepairable. We prayed with him for God's
guidance and assistance. Through another friend the next day, he
found a car for sale that met his needs and financial constraints.

The seller offered to fudge the selling price as a favor to
lower the transfer taxes. God had answered his prayer for an
affordable vehicle. Would he corrupt the blessing by cheating the
tax collector? God provided the money to purchase the car, as well
as the funds needed to transfer the title and auto tag. We wondered
if the seller was testing him. Unbelievers often try to trip us up. Or
perhaps he didn't understand Christian ethics.

Tempting though it was, our friend declined. If we stay on
our spiritual toes, we can avert the temptation to fall into the
"everybody does it" behavior. And at the same time, give a godly
testimony for Christ.

SCRIPTURE INDEX